EI 10/15

WITHDRAWN
2/8/23

CTC
TECHNOLOGY SECTION

CLEVELAND COLLEGE
LIBRARY

000 26325
536.2.

PHYSICS IN ENGINEERING 16 - 19

KU-508-312

CTC
TECHNOLOGY SECTION

PHYSICS IN ENGINEERING 16 - 19

MECHANICS AND HEAT

Gordon Raitt

Director
Physics in Engineering Project 16–19

Principal Sponsors

Royal Commission for the
Exhibition of 1851
Department of Trade
and Industry

CAMBRIDGE
UNIVERSITY PRESS

Published by the Press Syndicate of the University of Cambridge
The Pitt Building, Trumpington Street, Cambridge CB2 1RP
40 West 20th Street, New York, NY 10011–4211, USA
10 Stamford Road, Oakleigh, Victoria 3166, Australia

© Cambridge University Press 1992

First published 1992

Printed in Great Britain by Scotprint Ltd, Musselburgh

A catalogue record for this book is available from the British Library.

ISBN 0 521 36676 3 paperback

Cover design by Design/Section

Notice to teachers
The contents of this book are in the copyright of Cambridge University
Press. Unauthorised copying of any of the pages is not only illegal but also
goes against the interests of the author.
For authorised copying please check that your school has a licence (through
the local education authority) from the Copyright Licensing Agency which
enables you to copy small parts of the text in limited numbers.

Contents

Preface

The main aims

The main aims of the Physics in Engineering Project 16–19 and its books are:

- to show students ways in which the physics that they study is used in practice in industry and engineering;
- to provide numerical and other questions and problems that are based on the engineering that has been described;
- to convey a feel of what engineers do, and to interest students and teachers in engineering.

The content

The basis for the selection of the physics content has been the examination boards' joint publication *Common Cores at Advanced Level* (GCE Boards of England, Wales and Northern Ireland, 1983), with the object of ensuring that as much of the content as possible will be applicable to most students. The selection also relates closely to the Scottish Higher Grade Physics syllabus.

Engineering examples of the principles of physics can be found throughout engineering: in the aeronautical, automobile, civil, electrical, marine, mechanical and other fields. The selection has been determined mainly by the practicalities of what was accessible for visits from the work bases, and of what was amenable to development by correspondence with more distant engineering companies. Many more topics than those which appear were actually started and developed, but proved either too difficult in concepts or in presentation for this age group, or important information was ultimately not available. The ones that are printed provide a collection to act as examples.

Occasionally the work has been carried slightly beyond the indication in the Common Core. The chapter on mechanical vibrations is an example; mechanical vibrations occur and are of fundamental importance in all forms of engineering. Moreover, many of the basic concepts of waves and wave motion can be well seen and illustrated by mechanical vibrations.

The book is intended as a complement to the physics textbook that is in class use. It aims to show how physics that a class is studying is important in practice. The book does not set out to teach the physics, although sometimes a summary is provided.

The Physics in Engineering Project 16–19

The project is the follow-on to the 13–16 years School Physics in Engineering Project, with its five books published in 1987 under the series title *Physics in Action*. A 16–19 years follow-on was suggested at a meeting of the Physics Panel of the Industry Education Unit of the Department of Trade and Industry. The work is based on visits to manufacturing companies and to construction sites, on studies of firms' technical literature, and on correspondence with companies.

Acknowledgments

Funding was needed to enable visits to be made to companies during their working week, to enable extensive correspondence to be undertaken, and for the development work itself.

I am particularly grateful to The Fellowship of Engineering, London, and to the Ove Arup Partnership, Consulting Engineers, London, for their early interest in and financial support of the work; and to the Department of Trade and Industry, and the Royal Commission for the Exhibition of 1851 whose grants provided the main funding. Because the grants were on a joint funding basis, however, the work could not have been undertaken without the interest and financial support of other bodies and companies, and these are named below in the complete list of sponsors. To them I am very grateful.

APV Baker Limited
BICC plc
BOC Limited
British Steel
Department of Trade and Industry
The Electricity Council
The Fellowship of Engineering
Sir Alexander Gibb and Partners
Johnson Matthey
Kier Limited
The Mercers' Company
Ove Arup Partnership
Plessey Company
Royal Commission for the Exhibition of 1851
United Biscuits (UK) Limited
Wiggins Teape Group Limited

Two chapters are based on construction work studied during the building of a bridge, and I am very grateful to West Sussex County Council Engineers Department (design) and to Kier Limited (construction) for enabling me to make regular visits to the site over a two-year period. I am similarly grateful to the staffs of the firms that I visited.

The staffs of companies whose work or whose products are described have kindly read sections of the draft text and have made comments on these. Staff of Imperial College of Science and Technology Department of Civil Engineering and of the University of Reading Department of Engineering (both for mechanical vibrations) have helped similarly. These comments have enabled me to clarify and to improve a number of aspects, and I am very grateful to the members of the staffs.

Engineers and engineering

Throughout the years of the two projects, several features have been apparent again and again. There is an aesthetic beauty in design drawings, in machine parts, and in finished structures. Most machines operate with many physical principles and effects interacting at the same time and in complex ways; yet machines function smoothly day after day, month after month, often unseen and unnoticed beneath their cover. The staffs have encountered many difficulties and challenges in design and in manufacture, and have surmounted them. These staffs seem frequently to be modestly unaware of the greatness of their achievements. And British people seem sometimes not to recognise nor appreciate the vision, the imagination, the skills and the achievements of those who design and those who make. Their work is a central contribution to the life and the economy of Britain and of other nations.

Gordon Raitt
St Andrews

1. Stopping a moving load

Moving loads in industry

Figure 1.1 *A robot arm. The hand can be pulled in very rapidly, and can be stopped rapidly by decelerators at A and B. Decelerators at C and D decelerate an upward movement. What is the function of decelerator E? This figure is reproduced to a larger size on p. 11 (Source: ACE Controls International, Newton-le-Willows.)*

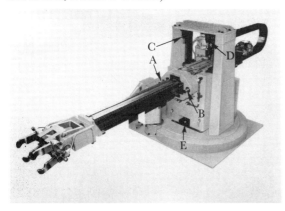

Almost all manufacturing processes involve movement of some kind. A component which is being moved from one place to another may have linear or rotary motion, a small or a large mass, and a small or a large velocity. Because of its mass and velocity, it possesses kinetic energy; if the body is to be stopped, this kinetic energy must be removed from it.

Also, if the moving body is to be stopped, its velocity must be reduced to zero; this means that it must be decelerated. For the body to be decelerated, an unbalanced force must be applied to it.

The ways in which the unbalanced force is applied and the kinetic energy is removed are each very important. Too great a force at the start of the deceleration can impose a shock on the component or equipment and can damage it. The mechanical handling equipment itself may be damaged. These damages cause stoppages, need for repairs, loss of production, and waste of money.

The kinetic energy of a moving body is given by

$$\text{Kinetic energy} = \tfrac{1}{2} mv^2$$

Thus the kinetic energy of a body is directly proportional to its mass, and proportional to the square of its velocity. A body of mass 2 kg moving with a velocity of $1 \, \text{m s}^{-1}$ has a kinetic energy of $\tfrac{1}{2} \times 2 \times 1^2$ joules $= 1 \, \text{J}$. The effects of doubling the mass and doubling the velocity are shown in Figure 1.2.

Figure 1.2 *The effect on kinetic energy of doubling the mass and doubling the velocity of a body.*

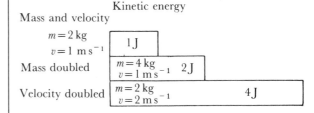

With increases in production rates and the increased use of automation, the velocities of components and equipment on production lines tend to be greater than before. These higher velocities can be achieved only if the bodies can be decelerated safely and their kinetic energy removed in a satisfactory way.

Figures 1.3, 1.4 and 1.5 show examples in which it was necessary to stop a moving mass safely. Figure 1.3(a) shows a process in which heavy drums were rolled down a ramp onto a conveyor belt where their right-to-left motion was stopped by rubber stops on a fixed vertical post. The rubber compressed by about 5 mm. Each drum was then carried away in a direction at right-angles to the original motion. The kinetic energy and velocity of each drum were such that the stops dented the drums and the post frequently broke near its foot.

Figure 1.3 *Heavy rolling drums are being brought to rest. In (a), the post was repeatedly broken; in (b), a specially designed decelerator was used. (Source: ACE Controls.)*

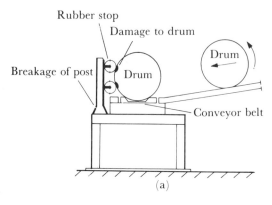

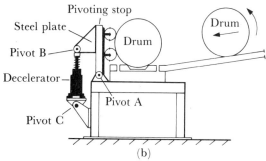

Figure 1.4 *A counterweight is used to aid the raising and lowering of a drill head. In (a), the counterweight chain repeatedly broke. (Source: ACE Controls.)*

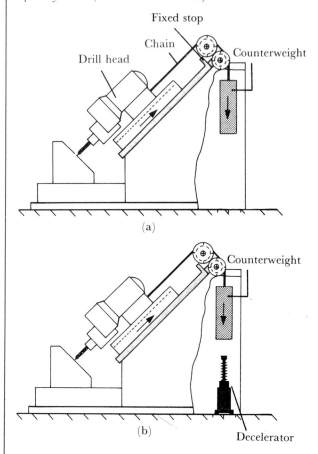

Figure 1.3(b) shows how a retarding force which acted over a greater distance was provided. The post was pivoted at pivot A, so that it could swing back. A triangular steel plate was fixed to the top of the post, and attached at pivot B to a device which would provide a retarding force. When a drum struck the rubber stops, the post pivoted at A and swung from right to left, this compressed the decelerator and provided a force in the opposite direction to the drum's motion.

The drum was decelerated to zero velocity through a distance of 75 mm, instead of the earlier 5 mm; and the drum then rolled back into the depression in the conveyor belt and was transported away. The drums and the post each remained undamaged.

1.1 Sketch the positions of the parts of the system when the post and rollers are in the pivoted back position.

Figure 1.4(a) shows a drill head which is raised and lowered hydraulically (not shown) and which has a counterweight to help this. When the drill head was raised, its baseplate hit the fixed stop and the drill unit was brought suddenly to rest. The counterweight continued its downward motion until the strain and stress in the chain arrested it. Repeated straining of the chain caused it to break from time to time, and then the drill unit slid down the ramp and drove the drill into the workpiece, damaging the drill and the work.

The problem was solved by placing under the counterweight a device which met the counterweight and provided a retarding force to its motion. The baseplate of the drill unit then approached the fixed stop at a low, safe velocity.

Figure 1.5 *The motion control arrangements for a gripper feeder and extractor in a metal press. (Source: ACE Controls.)*

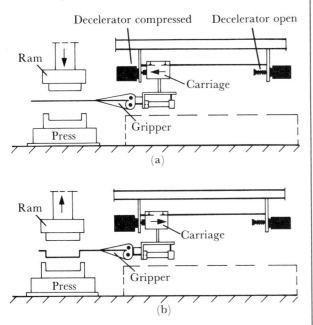

Springs

A spring may be used to provide the retarding force. Figure 1.6 shows a body of mass 1 kg moving at a velocity of $2\,\mathrm{m\,s^{-1}}$ from left to right on roller bearings. It meets the head of a piston attached to a spring and, compressing the spring, is brought to rest in a distance of 100 mm. The spring is compressed by the same amount, i.e. 100 mm.

The spring obeys Hooke's law, so the retarding force is proportional to the displacement. A graph of the retarding force provided by the spring against displacement is a straight line. When the mass has been brought to rest, the graph shows that the spring is exerting a force of 40 N on the body.

What will happen next?

The compressed spring is exerting a force on the body in the direction right to left, and its value is $-40\,\mathrm{N}$. The body is free to move on the rollers, and it is therefore accelerated by the force:

$$F = ma$$
$$-40 = 1 \times a$$
$$a = -40\,\mathrm{m\,s^{-2}}$$

The body is accelerated backwards at $40\,\mathrm{m\,s^{-2}}$, or about $4\,g$.

The spring stopped the moving body, but the kinetic energy of the body was not removed from the system; it became stored in the system as potential energy in the compressed spring. As the spring then accelerated the body backwards, and extended itself, potential energy was transformed into kinetic energy in the moving mass.

Let us consider the first stage, in which the body was stopped, and use the information in Figure 1.6:

$$\text{Kinetic energy} = \tfrac{1}{2}mv^2 = \tfrac{1}{2} \times 1 \times 2^2 \text{ joules} = 2\,\mathrm{J}$$

The work done on the spring in compressing it (and which is therefore stored in the compressed spring) is equal to the area under the curve from $s=0$ to $s=100$ mm. So

$$\begin{aligned}
\text{Work done} &= \text{area of the triangle} \\
&= \tfrac{1}{2}\,\text{height} \times \text{base} \\
&= \tfrac{1}{2} \times 40\,\mathrm{N} \times 0.1\,\mathrm{m} \\
&= 2\,\mathrm{N\,m} = 2\,\mathrm{J}
\end{aligned}$$

Usually it is necessary to bring a body to rest and leave it at rest so that an operation may be done on

Figure 1.5 shows a gripper feeder and extractor for a metal press. In (a) the gripper feeds a flat metal panel into the press, and allows the ram to press the panel. In (b) the gripper removes the pressed panel, and then conveys it on the carriage to the right-hand end of the structure.

The carriage must move forwards and backwards at high speed to maintain a high production rate. In the first design of the machine, when the carriage hit an end support there were high shock forces on the carriage and on the frame. This caused the gripper to misfeed the sheet into the press, causing stoppages, and resulting in a short life for the machine. The problem was solved by fixing a suitable decelerating device for the carriage at each end of the travel.

Decelerating a moving load

In order to decelerate a moving mass, an unbalanced force must be applied to it in the direction opposite to that of the motion.

Figure 1.6 *A moving mass being brought to rest by a spring, and the energy stored in the spring.*

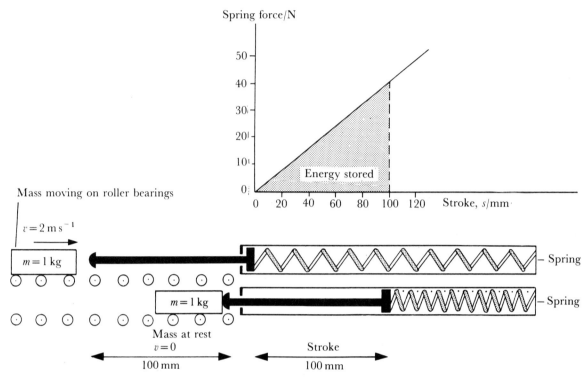

it. In these cases the use of a spring is not suitable. The spring stores energy and it may return the energy to the body, causing the body to start moving again, backwards.

Air cylinders

A moving load may be brought to rest by arranging for it to hit a piston and compress air sealed in a cylinder. Figure 1.7 shows such a pneumatic system. At the start, the air on each side of the piston is at 1 atmosphere pressure. As the moving load drives the piston from left to right, the pressure of the air rises in the right-hand compartment. The increasing pressure on the base of the piston produces an increasing force on the piston, in the right-to-left direction, and this decelerates the load.

The graph in Figure 1.7(a) shows that the pressure rises gently at first but very rapidly towards the end of the stroke. Thus the force on the body increases rapidly towards the end of the

stroke, and this can produce a shock effect. In industrial air cylinders, final pressures of 40 to 50 atmosphere are not unusual.

The kinetic energy of the body becomes transformed into potential energy stored in the compressed air. When the body has been brought to rest, if it is then free to move, the force from the compressed air will accelerate the body backwards, setting it in motion again. Like the spring decelerator, the pneumatic decelerator does not remove the kinetic energy from the system; it stores it as potential energy, and then returns it to the mass with resulting further motion.

Decelerating a body and removing kinetic energy

If a moving body is to be halted and then kept conveniently at rest, its energy of motion should be removed from the system altogether and not stored

Figure 1.7 *An air cylinder for stopping a moving load. (a) A graph of air pressure against stroke; (b) and (c) two positions of the piston.*

Figure 1.8 *The principle of an oil-filled piston: (a) at low piston velocity and laminar flow; (b) at high piston velocity and turbulent flow. In practice this design would not work.*

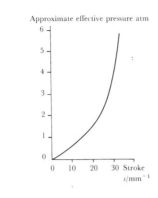

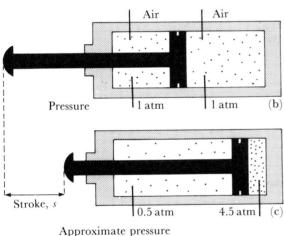

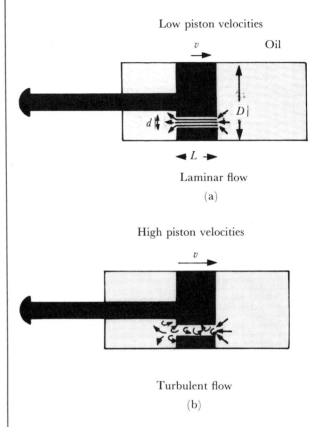

a velocity, the friction of the oil flowing through the channel raises the temperature of the oil. Heat is then lost to the outside.

If the external force on the piston is due to a free-moving body, then the friction force decelerates the piston and the body. When they are brought to rest, they remain at rest because the kinetic energy has been transformed into heat which is lost to the surroundings.

If the velocity of the oil through the hole is low, the fluid flow is streamlined, or laminar. The retarding force on the wall of the channel is then proportional to the velocity of the oil through the channel.

If the velocity of the oil through the hole is high, the fluid flow is turbulent; the retarding force on

in it. The most widely used means is to transform the kinetic energy into heat, and allow the heat to be lost into the atmosphere. The energy transformation can be done by using *fluid friction*.

Single orifice decelerators

Figure 1.8(a) shows a piston in a cylinder filled with oil. The piston has been drilled with a hole, or channel, through which the oil may flow from one compartment to the other. Oil is virtually incompressible. If a force is applied to the piston, giving it

the walls of the hole is then proportional to the fourth power of the oil velocity:

Laminar flow
Retarding force $\propto$ oil velocity

Turbulent flow
Retarding force $\propto$ (oil velocity)^4

In practice the device shown in Figure 1.8 would not work. Oil forced from the right-hand compartment must be accommodated in the left-hand compartment. If the piston were to move a distance S, the volume of oil displaced would be $\pi(\frac{1}{2}D)^2 S$, approximately. But the extra volume in the left-hand compartment would only be $\pi(\frac{1}{2}D)^2 S - \pi(\frac{1}{2}R)^2 S$, where R is the diameter of the piston rod. As the piston rod moves in, it occupies volume that the oil needs. Since the oil is incompressible, the result is that the piston cannot move.

In a practical shock absorber, extra volume must be made available to accommodate the oil displaced by the piston rod as it moves in.

Figure 1.9 *A practical design for an oil-filled decelerator. (Source: Enidine Industrial, Limited, Leighton Buzzard.)*

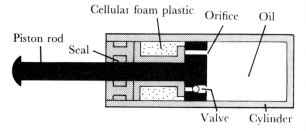

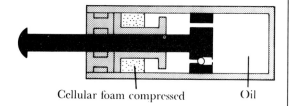

Figure 1.9 shows an arrangement for doing this. An additional compartment is provided which is filled with soft foamed elastomer. As oil is forced into the left-hand compartment, the soft cellular plastic becomes compressed and provides the extra volume that is needed.

1.2 At what stage in the piston movement is the retarding force at a maximum: early, middle, or late? Look back at the relations which give the retarding force.

Would you expect the retarding force to rise slowly or suddenly? Why?

Figure 1.10 *Curve of force against distance for an oil-filled decelerator with a single orifice. (After a diagram by Forkardt (England) Limited, Bristol.)*

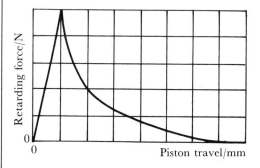

Figure 1.10 shows the general shape of the curve. For many practical purposes, the retarding force is too great in the early stage and too small in the later stage. The sudden rise of the retarding force to a high value can produce shock effects which can damage the body being decelerated.

Multiple orifice decelerators

A system is needed which produces a retarding force that is:

- small enough not to cause shock;
- reasonably constant for most of the stroke.

Figure 1.11 shows a device which meets these conditions.

1.3 Describe the working of the decelerator, using the following sequence.
  (a) Describe where the oil flows when the piston is forced in.
  (b) Are the orifice holes evenly spaced?
  (c) After the initial few millimetres of piston movement, does the retarding force on the piston remain reasonably constant?

Figure 1.11 *An oil-filled multiple orifice decelerator. (Source: Enidine Industrial, Limited.)*

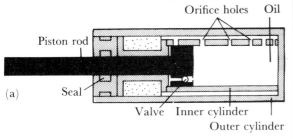

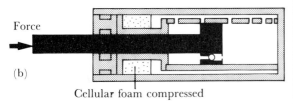

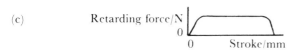

(d) What effect does this have on (i) the deceleration of the piston (and load); and (ii) the speed of the piston (and load)?

(e) Would the same effect be achieved by having all of the holes bored in the piston? (That would still be a multiple orifice decelerator.)

(f) Why is it that the system shown in Figure 1.11 is an improvement on that shown in Figure 1.9? Is it connected with the orifices not being evenly spaced? You may wish to look back at the relations on page 6.

(g) Would the force versus stroke curve look exactly as in Figure 1.11(c)? If not, sketch a more likely shape.

1.4 A load of mass *m* moving with a velocity *v* has to be brought to rest in a distance *S*. Four different methods are tried: a single orifice hydraulic device, a multiple orifice hydraulic device, an elastic medium such as a spring or a rubber buffer, and a pneumatic cylinder. Figure 1.12 shows the approximate curves for retarding force against stroke for these.

(a) For each system find the energy which is absorbed (and then either stored or given

Figure 1.12 *Curves of retarding force against piston movement (stroke) for different methods of decelerating the same load, moving at the same initial speed, and bringing it to a stop in the same distance. (After Forkardt (England) Ltd.)*

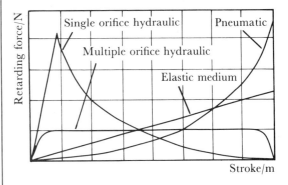

Figure 1.13 *Approximate graphs of piston velocity against stroke for three of the systems in Figure 1.12.*

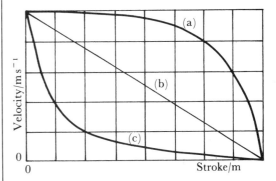

up). Do this by finding the approximate area under each curve, in terms of whole squares and tenths of squares.

(b) Comment on the results.

1.5 Figure 1.13 shows how the piston velocity changes as the stroke increases in three of the systems described for Figure 1.12. Compare these two diagrams and identify systems (a), (b) and (c).

1.6 A manufacturer (ACE Controls International) provides the following data for one of its hydraulic decelerators:

Overall length	330 mm
Overall diameter	75 mm
Piston diameter	30 mm

Piston stroke   100 mm
Mass   5.4 kg
Maximum average retarding force   27 000 N
Return spring force
   fully out   60 N
   fully compressed   170 N
Piston return time   0.6 s
Maximum energy capacity per hour
   as shown in Figure 1.14   230 000 J
   with circulated oil cooling   7 200 000 J
Maximum operating temperature,
   with standard oil and standard oil seals   90 °C
   with special oil and special oil seals   120 °C

Notes: (1) The maximum energy capacity is based on an atmospheric temperature of 20 °C. (2) The steel body has a black oxide finish; do not paint over the body.

(a) Practical decelerators have a return spring. What is its function?

(b) When the piston is stopping a moving load, does the return spring make any significant contribution?

(c) How much work is done in compressing the return spring through the stroke?

(d) How much work does the compressed spring do in returning the piston to its normal position?

(e) What power is the spring providing in (d)?

(f) What is the maximum power that the decelerator in Figure 1.14 can absorb from moving loads?

(g) The decelerator in Figure 1.14 is to be connected to an oil cooling system. When this is done, and the arrangement is working at its maximum capacity, what power will be given up to the atmosphere?

Figure 1.14 *Overall dimensions for a company's Model $1\frac{1}{8} \times 4$ hydraulic decelerator. (Source: ACE Controls.)*

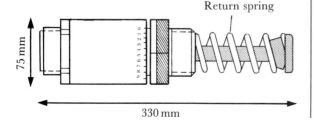

(h) What factors appear to limit the upper temperature at which the decelerator can work?

(i) When calculating or finding experimentally the maximum energy capacity, why it is necessary to state an atmospheric temperature?

(j) What is the significance of note (2)?

Figure 1.15 *A load of mass m moving with a speed v on roller bearings is to be brought to rest in a distance s. (Source: ACE Controls.)*

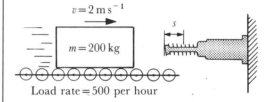

Let us calculate the power to be removed in stopping a succession of moving loads, and consider the temperature rise of the decelerator (Figure 1.15). Boxes, each with a mass of 200 kg, move along roller bearings at a speed of 2.0 m s^{-1} and are brought to rest by a decelerator. The boxes arrive and are stopped at a rate of 500 per hour.

What is the power that has to be absorbed by the decelerator? This power then has to be given out to the atmosphere in the form of heat:

$$\text{Kinetic energy of each load} = \tfrac{1}{2} mv^2$$
$$= \tfrac{1}{2} \times 200 \times 2.0^2 \text{ joules} = 400 \text{ J}$$
$$\therefore \text{ Energy to be absorbed per hour} = 500 \times 400 \text{ J}$$

$$\therefore \text{ Energy to be absorbed per second}$$
$$= \frac{500 \times 400 \text{ J}}{60 \times 60 \text{ s}} = 56 \text{ J s}^{-1} = 56 \text{ W}$$

What would be the temperature rise of the decelerator per hour if it were insulated and did not lose heat to the atmosphere?

A manufacturer of multiple orifice oil-filled decelerators says that for this particular job its Model A $1\frac{1}{8} \times 4$ would be suitable. The volume of oil is 66 cm^3, giving a mass of 58 g; and the mass of steel is 5.4 kg. The specific heat capacities are: oil, 1900 J kg^{-1} K^{-1}; and steel, 470 J kg^{-1} K^{-1}.

The energy absorbed by a body because of a rise $\Delta\theta$ in its temperature is:

Energy absorbed
= mass × specific heat capacity × temperature rise
= $mc\Delta\theta$

In this situation:

Energy absorbed $= m_{\text{oil}}c_{\text{oil}}\Delta\theta + m_{\text{steel}}c_{\text{steel}}\Delta\theta$
$= (m_{\text{oil}}c_{\text{oil}} + m_{\text{steel}}c_{\text{steel}})\Delta\theta$
$= (0.058 \times 1900 + 5.4 \times 470)\Delta\theta$
$= (110 + 2540)\Delta\theta$ joules
$= 2650\Delta\theta$ joules

Kinetic energy supplied by moving loads per hour	= energy absorbed by shock absorber per hour
400×500 joules	$= 2650\Delta\theta$ joules
$\dfrac{400 \times 500}{2650}$	$= \Delta\theta$
giving $\Delta\theta$	$= 75$
Temperature rise	$= 75$ K

Therefore, if the decelerator were perfectly insulated, its temperature would rise by 75 K per hour.

In practice, the decelerator would be exposed to the atmosphere. Its temperature would rise until the rate of loss of heat from the decelerator surface to the atmosphere (by conduction, convection and radiation) equalled the rate of supply of energy to the decelerator by the moving loads. The decelerator would then remain at a steady temperature above atmospheric temperature.

The manufacturer states that if the user wishes to fit a smaller, more compact and lighter decelerator to do the same job, then model AA $\frac{3}{4} \times 3$ could be used. It would be only $\frac{1}{4}$ m in length instead of $\frac{1}{3}$ m, and its mass would be only 2 kg instead of over 5 kg. But it would operate at a much higher temperature, the temperature would be too high, and this smaller shock absorber would have to be fitted with an oil cooling system.

1.7 In the operation which is shown in Figure 1.15, page 8, the decelerator stroke was 100 mm. That is, the load was brought to rest in a distance of 100 mm.
(a) What was the average retarding force on the load, taking the direction of travel as positive?
(b) What was the average acceleration of the load?
(c) Approximately how many g is the acceleration?
(d) Examining the appropriate curve in Figure 1.12, would you say that the retarding force ever rose significantly above the value you calculated in (a)?

1.8 An industrial operation is carried out by the same arrangement as shown in Figure 1.15, but in this case the load is metal ingots, each with a mass of 400 kg, moving on roller bearings at a speed of 1.8 m s^{-1}, and they are brought to rest at a rate of 600 ingots per hour.
(a) Calculate the power, in watts, which the decelerator has to absorb.
(b) The decelerator is made of steel with a mass of 2.0 kg and contains 20 g of oil. The specific heat capacity of the steel is 470 J kg^{-1} K^{-1}, and that of the oil is 1900 J kg^{-1} K^{-1}. If the decelerator were perfectly insulated, through what temperature would it rise in 1 hour? (For this job, the bare decelerator would in practice need an oil cooling system.)

1.9 Figure 1.16 shows a body being conveyed on rollers which are driven round by a motor. The rotating rollers remain in fixed positions. When each body has been brought to rest by the decelerator, the rollers continue to turn underneath it. The stationary body is then removed.
The coefficient of sliding friction, μ, between the rollers and the body is 0.20.

Figure 1.16 A mass being conveyed by rollers which are driven round on axles, whose positions remain fixed. (Source: ACE Controls.)

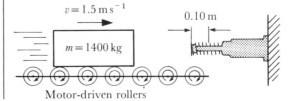

Sliding friction force = μ × force normal to the two surfaces in contact

The decelerator stroke is 0.10 m, in bringing the moving load to rest.

(a) How much energy does the decelerator have to absorb in bringing one body to rest? (Calculate the kinetic energy of the mass, and the work done by the rollers in moving the body through a distance of 0.10 m.)

(b) If the operation is being done 180 times per hour, what is the power that the decelerator has to transfer to the atmosphere?

1.10

(a) In Figure 1.17, say what you think is the purpose of the system.

(b) Describe how it works.

(c) When the piston has been forced in, by what means is it returned to its normal position?

1.11

Figure 1.18 is a cathode ray oscillograph for a decelerator, showing the retarding force at different stages of the stroke.

(a) Why does the trace fall and rise successively?

(b) How many orifices are there in the decelerator?

(c) Are the orifices evenly spaced?

(d) Is the retarding force reasonably constant for most of the stroke?

1.12

(a) In Figure 1.19 find:
(i) the piston; (ii) the inner fluid compartment; (iii) orifices; (iv) the outer fluid compartment.

(b) Examine Figure 1.15. The decelerator has been chosen so as to be well suited to masses of 200 kg moving at $2 \, \text{m s}^{-1}$. If the next

Figure 1.17 *What is this system? How does it work? (Source: ACE Controls.)*

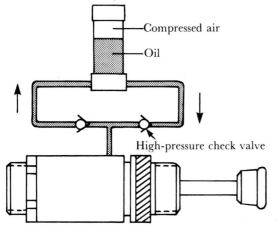

Figure 1.19 *Cut-away section of an adjustable hydraulic decelerator. (Source: Forkardt (England) Limited.)*

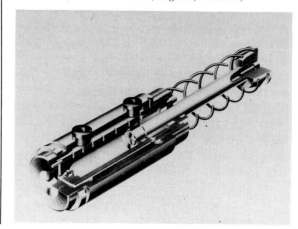

Figure 1.18 *A cathode ray oscillograph for the motion of a decelerator. (Source: ACE Controls.)*

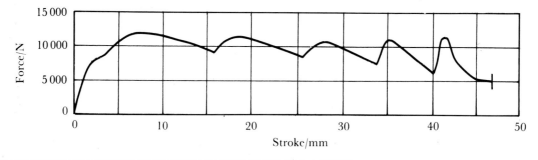

batch of work involved masses of 20 kg moving at $1.4 \, \mathrm{m\,s^{-1}}$, would the decelerator necessarily give the best deceleration?

(c) To avoid having to replace a decelerator each time a production process is changed, manufacturers have devised adjustable decelerators. These can be altered to provide different average forces during the stroke. What quantities in a decelerator design could be altered to alter its performance? Check Figure 1.8, on page 5.

(d) Which quantity or quantities might be made variable without dismantling the device?

(e) In Figure 1.19, which quantity has the manufacturer decided to make adjustable?

How is it done? Figure 1.14 gives further information.

Answers to text questions

1.4 Energy converted is represented by approximately 8 squares.

1.5 (a) Pneumatic; (b) Multiple orifice hydraulic; (c) Single orifice hydraulic.

1.6 (c) 12 J; (d) 12 J; (e) 20 W; (f) 64 W; (g) 2.0 kW.

1.7 (a) $-4000 \, \mathrm{N}$; (b) $-20 \, \mathrm{m\,s^{-2}}$; (c) -2; (d) No.

1.8 (a) 110 W; (b) 400 K per hour.

1.9 (a) 1900 J; (b) 93 W.

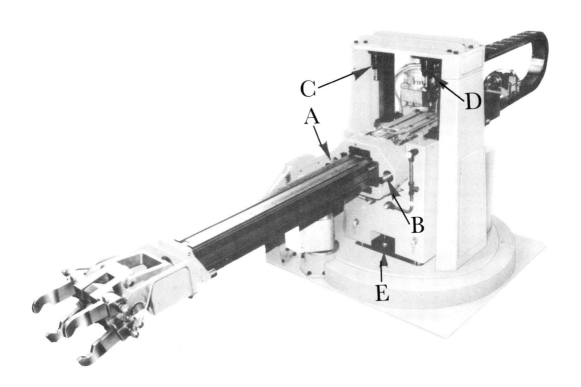

2. Mechanical vibrations

Figure 2.1 *Part of a dismantled roller bearing system. On the left is the outer race; on the right is the inner race. Three rollers are also shown. The outer race is badly pitted, probably through corrosion. During rotation, rollers in succession struck the pits and set up vibrations. (Source: Bruel and Kjaer, Limited.)*

Figure 2.2 *(a) Shaft rotating in a roller bearing. There is a fault in the outer race. (b) Shock pulses as rollers in succession hit the fault. (c) The main vibration frequency is 5 kHz.*

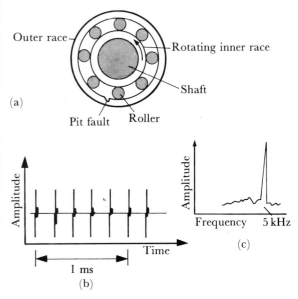

All structures and all machines vibrate, some a little and some a lot. Vibration is therefore an important aspect of engineering, and engineers have to consider vibration from the design stage of their work, through production to operation in service.

Some sources of vibrations

A rotating shaft must be supported; this is done by means of bearings. Figure 2.1 shows part of a dismantled roller bearing system. The bearing was vibrating to an unacceptable level and had to be dismantled. When this was done, the outer race was found to be badly pitted; these pits had been causing vibrations.

Figure 2.2 indicates how a fault in a bearing can set up vibrations. The diagram in (a) shows a shaft and the inner race rotating. This rotation causes

the rollers to move round. But there is a small pit in the outer race. In moving round the race, the rollers successively land in the pit and set up a succession of shock waves, which cause the vibration. The graph in (b) shows how the amptitude of the vibration varies with time. There is a series of shock pulses as a roller hits the pit and momentarily displaces the outer race outwards. There are 5 pulses in 1 ms, that is, 5000 pulses in 1 s, giving a vibration frequency of 5000 Hz. Figure 2.2(c) shows an analysis of the vibration amplitude at different frequencies. There is a marked peak at 5 kHz, that is 5000 Hz; other frequencies are also present.

Power is often transferred by means of shafts and gears. When a tooth on one gear meshes with a tooth on the second gear the forces on the gears change. With gears rotating and teeth meshing

Figure 2.3 *Rotating gears. When teeth mesh from two rotating gears there is a series of impacts, and vibrations are produced. (Source: Bruel and Kjaer Limited.)*

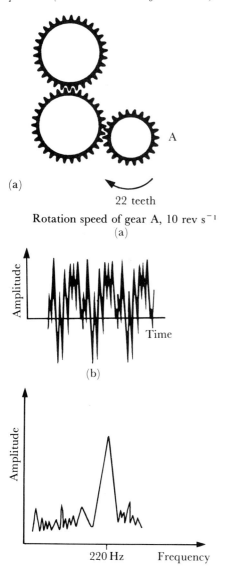

(a)

22 teeth

Rotation speed of gear A, 10 rev s⁻¹

(a)

(b)

(c)

220 Hz   Frequency

Figure 2.3(b) shows how the vibration amplitude in the gears changes with time. Figure 2.3(c) shows the vibration amplitude at different frequencies; there is a marked peak at 220 Hz. Other frequencies are also present.

A shaft cannot be made so that it is exactly balanced about its axis. The centre of mass of a straight shaft is always very slightly off the axis of the shaft. When the shaft is rotated, the off-axis centre of mass produces cyclic forces on the bearings. These cyclic forces produce vibration. (Forces due to unbalanced rotors are discussed in Chapter 3.)

Figure 2.4(a) shows a rotating shaft. The imbalance in the shaft, and the slight distortion of the shape of the shaft from that of a long cylinder, are causing the support to vibrate. Figure 2.4(b) shows the variation of vibration amplitude with time, and (c) shows how the amplitude changes with frequency.

The shaft rotation speed is 2400 rev min⁻¹, which is 40 rev s⁻¹. The frequency graph in (c) shows a high peak at 40 Hz. A rotating shaft produces vibrations with a vibration frequency which is equal to the shaft rotation frequency.

In practice, most systems of machinery consist of several moving parts: a motor or engine; a transmission system; and the equipment needed to perform the operation. Each of these moving parts will produce vibrations.

Figure 2.5(a) shows such a system. An electric motor is driving a compressor; Figure 2.5(b) shows the numbered parts. (1) is the electric motor and (6) is the compressor. The two are connected by a transmission system which consists of a short shaft (2), a coupling (3), two gears (4), and an axle which is mounted in bearings (5).

The compressor produces a low-frequency vibration, A. The rotating shaft produces a vibration at the shaft rotation frequency, B. A loose coupling will produce vibrations at $2 \times$ shaft rotation frequency (C). The two gears produce vibrations at the tooth meshing frequency (D); and faults in the bearings produce vibrations at frequencies of E_1 and E_2.

Figure 2.6 shows the principal parts in an ethylene compressor. The compressor consists of six rotors with blades, mounted on a shaft.

alternately, the gears vibrate. The vibration frequency is equal to the tooth meshing frequency.

In Figure 2.3(a), gear A has 22 teeth and is rotating at 10 rev s⁻¹. Therefore in each second there are 10×22 meshing contacts between teeth, i.e. 220 contacts. The vibration frequency which is produced is 220 vibrations per second, or 220 Hz.

Figure 2.4 *A rotating shaft and its vibration pattern. (Source: Bruel and Kjaer Limited.)*

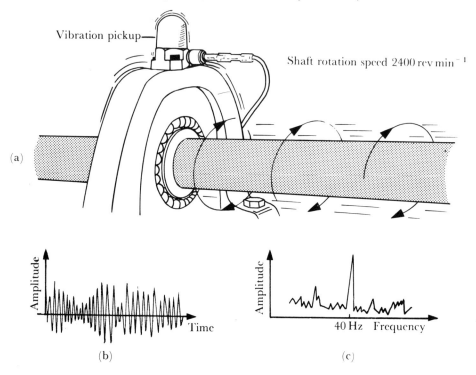

Figure 2.5 *An electric motor driving a compressor through a short shaft and gears. (Source: Bruel and Kjaer Limited.)*

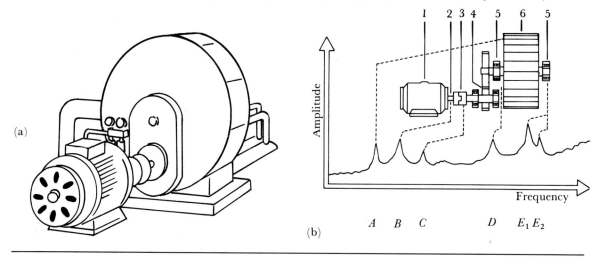

Figure 2.6 *A high-pressure compressor for ethylene gas in a petrochemical plant. (Source: Bruel and Kjaer Limited.)*

Machine details and characteristic frequencies

Plant: Petrochem   Section: Ethylene
Machine Nos: 2 R1 HP   **(High-pressure compressor)**

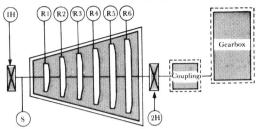

2.1

(a) Find the six rotors, R1 (with 23 blades) to R6 (with 29 blades).

(b) Find the shaft, S, which supports the rotors.

(c) Find the bearings which support the shaft: front end bearing, 1H; and back end bearing, 2H.

(d) Find the gearbox.

2.2 Make a list of the parts which might produce vibrations.

Table 2.1. Frequencies for some parts of the compressor system illustrated in Figure 2.6

Shaft rotation frequency	Gears			Rotors		
RPM	Gear no.	No. of teeth	Mesh frequency (Hz)	Rotor no.	No. blades	Bladepass frequency (Hz)
3500	1	23	1342	R1	23	1342
	2	16		R2	25	1458
				R3	25	1458
				R4	27	
				R5	27	
				R6	29	

(*Source:* Bruel and Kjaer Limited.)

2.3 Table 2.1 gives some frequency data for the compressor in Figure 2.6.

(a) What is the rotation frequency of the shaft, in hertz?

(b) What is the meshing frequency of gear number 2 (which meshes with gear number 1)?

(c) For the rotors, what do you think 'Bladepass frequency' means?

(d) What are the bladepass frequencies for rotors R4, R5 and R6?

2.4 Sketch axes for a graph such as that shown in Figure 2.5. Mark the *y*-axis 'Amplitude' and the *x*-axis 'Vibration frequency'. On the *x*-axis, sketch in a frequency scale up to 1700 Hz.

A vibration meter is fixed on the top of a bearing housing in the machine in Figure 2.6, and measurements of vibration amplitude are made up to a frequency of 1700 Hz.

Sketch the graph that you would expect from plotting the measurements. (The most pronounced vibrations are likely to be produced by the rotors.)

Vibration parameters

Figure 2.7 *A vibrating bar, fixed at one end and free at the other end. The curves show how the displacement of the free end of the bar, its velocity, and its acceleration change with time, t. (Source: Bruel and Kjaer Limited.)*

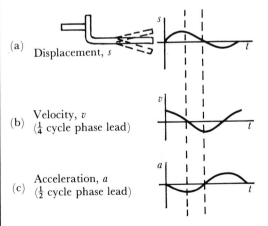

(a) Displacement, *s*

(b) Velocity, *v* ($\frac{1}{4}$ cycle phase lead)

(c) Acceleration, *a* ($\frac{1}{2}$ cycle phase lead)

The parameters by which mechanical vibrations are measured are *displacement* (*s*, measured in metres, millimetres or micrometres), *velocity* (*v*, measured in metres per second or millimetres per second), *acceleration* (*a*, measured in metres per second^2 or millimetres per second^2), and *frequency* (*f*, measured in vibrations per second, Hz).

If the *displacement* of a part of the system follows a simple harmonic motion, then the graph of displacement against time is a sine curve.

The graph of the velocity of the same part against time and the graph of the acceleration of the part against time are also sine curves. These three curves all have the same frequency, but there is a phase difference.

This is shown in Figure 2.7. In (a) a bar is shown fixed at one end and free at the other end. The free end is vibrating in a vertical plane about its rest position, which is also the mean position. At time $t = 0$, the displacement $s = 0$. As t increases, the displacement increases in the positive direction. When the end of the bar has reached its maximum displacement, s, it comes to rest and the velocity is zero, $v = 0$. This is shown in graph (a) and graph (b).

Considering Figure 2.7(a) again, when the end of the rod begins to move downwards, its speed increases, and the speed becomes maximum at the instant when the rod passes through the mean position. At that instant the displacement, s, is zero, and the velocity, v, is a maximum.

There is a phase difference between the displacement and the velocity. They are out of phase by $\frac{1}{4}$ of a cycle.

Looking at Figure 2.7(b), one sees that when $t = 0$, the velocity is a maximum in the positive direction, and is about to decrease. It is doing what the displacement will be doing $\frac{1}{4}$ of a cycle later. So the velocity phase is ahead of the displacement phase by $\frac{1}{4}$ of a cycle.

Examine Figure 2.7 (a) and (c):

2.5 Consider how the vibrating bar behaves, and work out at what stages in the motion the acceleration is greatest and at what stage it is zero.

2.6 Describe the acceleration as the displacement changes. Show that there is a phase difference of $\frac{1}{2}$ cycle. Show that the acceleration phase is $\frac{1}{2}$ cycle ahead of the displacement phase.

The magnitude of a vibration can be described by its amplitudes. A vibration has a displacement amplitude, a velocity amplitude, and an acceleration amplitude.

In Figure 2.8, the *frequency*, in Hz, is given on the horizontal axis; the scale is logarithmic. The acceleration of the body is given on the vertical axis; on the left it is given in SI units, and on the right it is given in terms of the acceleration due to gravity, $g = 10 \, \mathrm{m\,s^{-2}}$. The scale is logarithmic.

The dotted lines indicate typical maximum displacement of the body from the mean position; and the dashed lines indicate velocity. (The velocity figures are root mean square velocity values.)

A small diagram on the left-hand side of the nomogram shows part of a ship's rail and a passenger feeling unwell. The ship may be moving vertically up and down, or it may be rolling through an angle. Imagine one of these motions. From the scale on the horizontal axis we see that a typical frequency for the motion would be about 0.2 Hz. The *period* of the motion, the time required to perform one complete vibration, would therefore be about 5 s; period = 1/frequency.

From the scale on the vertical axis we see that the maximum acceleration of the passenger could lie in the range $100 \, \mathrm{mm\,s^{-2}}$ $(0.01 \, g)$ to $1 \, \mathrm{m\,s^{-2}}$ $(0.1 \, g)$. (Accelerations below $1 \, \mathrm{m\,s^{-2}}$ $(0.1 \, g)$ are marked on the right-hand side of the nomogram.) From the dotted lines we see that the maximum displacement from the mean position, the displacement amplitude, could lie in the range of a few millimetres to a few metres.

2.7 From the dashed lines, in what range might the vibration velocity lie?

A person who is standing on a floor that is vibrating vertically is sensitive to vibrations with a frequency of about 10 Hz. Amplitudes of about 100 micrometres are readily sensed and cause discomfort. This is shown on the nomogram.

2.8 What is the approximate acceleration range for such vibrations?

2.9 Alternating current electrical machinery vibrates at a frequency that is related to the frequency of the alternating current. In the nomogram, comment on the vibration frequency of the transformer, and the vibration frequency of the large electric motor.

Figure 2.8 *A nomogram, which, for vibrations, links their frequency, displacement amplitude, velocity amplitude, and acceleration amplitude. (The velocity figures are root mean square velocity values.) (Adapted from a nomogram of Bruel and Kjaer Limited.)*

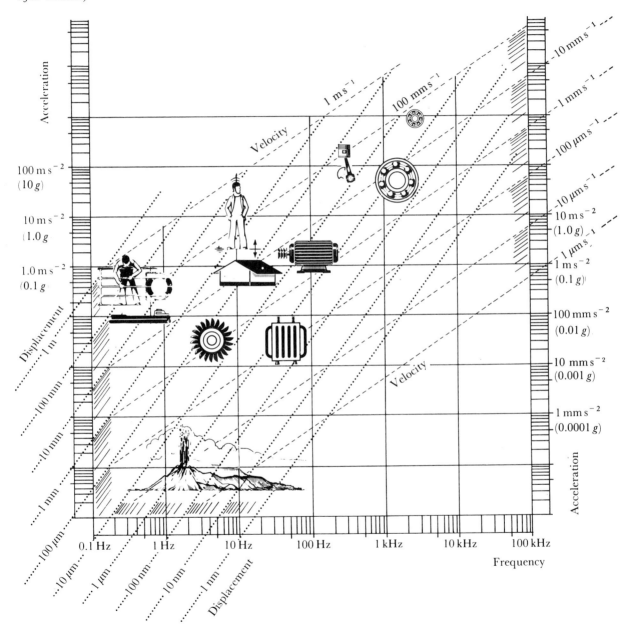

2.10 The nomogram shows two ball-bearing units. For one of these, describe the vibrations by referring to the parameters and their magnitudes.

Mathematical relationships between the vibration parameters

If the vibration is a simple harmonic one, then the displacement, x, at any time, t, is related to the displacement amplitude, r, by the equation

$$x = r \sin \omega t \tag{1}$$

where ω is the angular velocity of the radius vector that describes the motion; ω is related to the frequency, f, of the vibration by the equation

$$\omega = 2\pi f \tag{2}$$

The velocity, v, of the vibrating body or part is the rate of change of its displacement, x. Thus

$$v = \frac{dx}{dt} = \frac{d}{dt}(r \sin \omega t)$$

$$= \omega r \cos \omega t \tag{3}$$

The acceleration, a, of the vibrating body or part is the rate of change of its velocity, v. Thus

$$a = \frac{dv}{dt} = \frac{d}{dt}(\omega r \cos \omega t)$$

$$= -\omega \omega r \sin \omega t$$
$$= -\omega^2 r \sin \omega t \tag{4}$$

Summarising, and using equation (2),

$x = r \sin \omega t$	$x = r \sin \omega t$	(a)
$v = \omega r \cos \omega t$	$v = 2\pi f r \cos \omega t$	(b)
$a = -\omega^2 r \sin \omega t$	$a = -4\pi^2 f^2 r \sin \omega t$	(c)

The displacement, velocity, and acceleration are therefore out of phase with each other. The velocity is 90° out of phase with the displacement.

From equations (a) and (c) it might at first sight appear that the displacement, x, and the acceleration, a, are in phase with each other; each contains the term $\sin \omega t$. But when the displacement x is increasing in one direction, the *negative sign* in the acceleration expression shows that the acceleration,

a, is increasing in magnitude in the *opposite* direction. The two are thus 180° or $\frac{1}{2}$ cycle out of phase.

We can find the parameter amplitudes, or *maximum values*, from equations (a), (b), and (c). The displacement x, will be at a maximum when $\sin \omega t = 1$. The velocity, v, will be at a maximum when $\cos \omega t = 1$. The acceleration, a, will be at a maximum when $\sin \omega t = 1$. Therefore

Displacement amplitude,	$x_{max} = r$	(i)
Velocity amplitude,	$v_{max} = 2\pi f r$	(ii)
Acceleration amplitude,	$a_{max} = 4\pi^2 f^2 r$	(iii)

2.11 Do equations (i), (ii), and (iii) give values that are consistent with the figures given in the nomogram in Figure 2.8? Check for the large electric motor in the nomogram. Find its vibration frequence, f, and its displacement amplitude, r. Substitute these values in equation (ii) to obtain a value for the velocity amplitude, v_{max}. How does this value of v_{max} compare with the value read from the nomogram? Is it approximately the same, or very different?

Use equation (iii) to obtain a value for the acceleration amplitude a_{max}. How does this value compare with that obtained from the nomogram?

Measuring instruments

The most widely used device for measuring vibration magnitudes is the *piezoelectric accelerometer*. This measures the acceleration of the vibration; and the result can be used to obtain the vibration velocity and the vibration displacement.

Certain materials are piezoelectric. If a force is applied to opposite sides of the material, a separation of charge occurs; one side becomes positively charged and the other side negatively charged. Figure 2.9(a) and (b) shows the effect.

The force on the material distorts the crystal lattice, which produces the separation of charge.

Certain naturally occurring minerals are piezoelectric, particularly quartz crystals and tourmaline crystals. Man-made piezoelectric materials often contain lead zirconate and lead titanate, and they are usually manufactured in ceramic form.

Figure 2.9 *A piezoelectric crystal. A force on the crystal produces a separation of charge. A changing force produces a changing charge separation.*

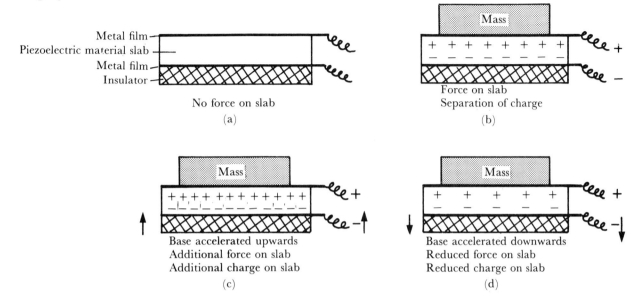

The piezoelectric effect can be used to measure *force* and to measure *acceleration*. Figure 2.9 shows the principle of the method. A metal film, usually silver, is deposited on opposite faces of a thin slab of piezoelectric material. An electrical connection is made to each metal film. The metallised slab is supported on an insulator. In Figure 2.9(b) a mass has been placed on the piezoelectric slab. The compressive force on the slab distorts the crystal lattice and causes a separation of charge. This generates an electromotive force (emf) between the opposite faces of the slab, and the effect can be detected and measured.

The charge separation, and thus the emf, are directly proportional to the stress (the force per unit area) on the slab.

In Figure 2.9(c), the base is being accelerated upwards. In order for the upper mass to accelerate, an additional force must be applied to it. This force is transmitted from the base through the slab to the mass. The result is an additional compression of the slab, an additional separation of charge, and an increased emf.

The additional force on the mass is proportional to the acceleration, that is, $F \propto a$. But the charge separation is proportional to the force per unit area.

Thus the charge separation is proportional to the acceleration, and

Electrical output $\propto$ acceleration

Figure 2.10 shows a simplified design for a piezoelectric accelerometer. A mass is placed above a thin slab of piezoelectric material, with its metallised upper and lower surfaces. The mass is held in place by a retaining spring. Electrical leads from the metallised top and bottom of the slab are

Figure 2.10 *Diagramatic representation of a piezoelectric accelerometer.*

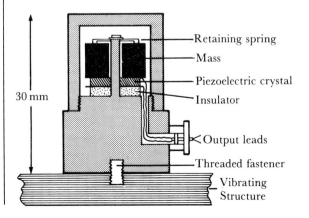

connected to the output. The body of the accelerometer is fixed to the vibrating structure by a screw stud fastener.

These accelerometers are designed and manufactured to produce a compact, lightweight device. A typical accelerometer for general vibration testing and control is shown in Figure 2.1; the accelerometer is the squat device on the right-hand side of the photograph. It is about 30 mm in length.

The manufacturer's data for the accelerometer in Figure 2.1 is

Charge sensitivity $1\,\mathrm{pC}/(\mathrm{m\,s}^{-2})$
Frequency range $0.1\,\mathrm{Hz}$–$12\,000\,\mathrm{Hz}$

Voltage sensitivity $0.8\,\mathrm{mV}/(\mathrm{m\,s}^{-2})$
Mass   16 grams

2.12 If the accelerometer is subjected to an acceleration of $10\,\mathrm{m\,s}^{-2}$ $(1\,g)$ what charge separation takes place?

2.13 The accelerometer is fixed to a vibrating structure and connected to a charge amplifier and read-out. The maximum charge separation indicates 2.5 pC. What is the acceleration amplitude of the vibration?

Calculating velocity and displacement from acceleration

A vibration accelerometer can be used to obtain vibration velocity and vibration displacement. If the acceleration is integrated with respect to time, then the velocity is obtained:

Acceleration = rate of change of velocity

$$a = \frac{\mathrm{d}v}{\mathrm{d}t}$$

$$\therefore\ a\mathrm{d}t = \mathrm{d}v$$

and

$$\int a\mathrm{d}t = v$$

If the velocity is integrated with respect to time, the displacement is obtained:

Velocity = rate of change of displacement

$$v = \frac{\mathrm{d}x}{\mathrm{d}t}$$

$$\therefore\ v\mathrm{d}t = \mathrm{d}x$$

and

$$\int v\mathrm{d}t = x$$

These integrations can be done electronically. The vibration meter illustrated in Figures 2.1 and 2.12 includes an integrator.

In Figure 2.12, the technician is making a record of the vibration level of rotating machinery. An

Figure 2.12 A vibration measuring system. An accelerometer is mounted on the vibrating machinery. The technician is holding an integrating vibration meter, which indicates vibration acceleration and vibration velocity. (Source: Bruel and Kjaer Limited.)

Figure 2.11 The main parts in a vibration meter.

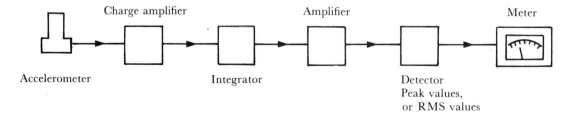

Accelerometer   Charge amplifier   Integrator   Amplifier   Detector Peak values, or RMS values   Meter

accelerometer and its attached charge amplifier are mounted on the upper surface of an electric motor. The hand-held meter is battery-operated and contains the integrator and the subsequent stages shown in Figure 2.11.

The manufacturer's data for the assembly is

Frequency range	10 Hz–10 000 Hz
Acceleration range	1 m s^{-2}–1000 m s^{-2}
	(0.1 g–100 g)
Velocity range	0.1 mm s^{-1}–100 mm s^{-1}

Natural frequencies and mode shapes

Any system which has mass and elasticity can be made to vibrate. Since all mechanical systems have mass and elasticity, they will all vibrate under certain conditions.

If a mechanical system is distorted by the application of a force, and then released by removal of the force, the system will vibrate at one or more of its *natural frequencies*.

Figure 2.13(a) shows a thin beam. It is fixed firmly at its left-hand end. In (a)(i) the free end has been pulled upwards and then released. The freed end springs downwards and the elements of the beam vibrate about their rest positions.

The beam is vibrating at a *natural vibration frequency*; there are no external forces acting on the vibrating parts.

In (a) the vibration pattern is the simplest that the beam can have, and the vibration frequency is the lowest natural one. The vibration pattern is the *first vibration mode*, and the frequency is the *fundamental frequency* of the beam, when it is fixed as shown.

Figure 2.13(a)(iv) shows the extreme positions and the rest position. The fixed end of the beam does not vibrate when the other parts of the beam are vibrating; it is at *a node*.

The beam can be made to vibrate vertically in other ways. Figure 2.13(b)(i)–(iv) shows the next pattern, the *second vibration mode*. There are *two nodes*, one where the beam is fixed and the other near the free end. The vibration frequency is different from that in the first mode, and is known as the *second natural frequency*.

Figure 2.13 *Vibration modes of a thin beam which is fixed at the left-hand end. In (a) the free end has been pulled upwards, and then released. The beam then vibrates about its rest position.*

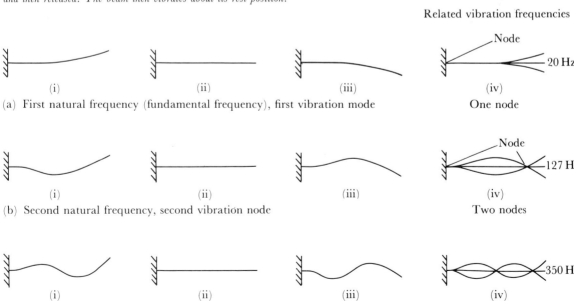

Related vibration frequencies

(a) First natural frequency (fundamental frequency), first vibration mode — One node — 20 Hz

(b) Second natural frequency, second vibration node — Two nodes — 127 Hz

(c) Third natural frequency, third vibration mode — Three nodes — 350 Hz

Figure 2.13(c) shows the *third vibration mode*, at the *third natural frequency*. There are three nodes.

Figure 2.13 also gives the vibration frequencies for one particular beam. There is a relationship between these frequencies; but it is not a simple ratio.

The vibration frequency, *f*, of the beam depends upon the *mass*, *m*, of the beam, the *dimensions*, and *Young's modulus of elasticity*, *E*, of the beam:

$$f = C \times S \times \frac{1}{2\pi}\sqrt{\left(\frac{E}{m}\right)} \qquad (1)$$

where *C* = mode constant and *S* = beam shape and dimensions quantity.

Young's modulus of elasticity of a material is a measure of the *stiffness* of the material, that is, of its ability to resist elastic deformation. The higher the value of *E*, the stiffer the material.

2.14 Supply the missing words in the following sentences. For a cantilever beam such as that in Figure 3.12:
The greater the stiffness of the beam, the .... the vibration frequency.
The greater the mass of the beam, the ....
the vibration frequency.

For a cantilever beam, using equation (1), the values of the mode constants are

Mode 1, *C* = 3.52
Mode 2, *C* = 22.4
Mode 3, *C* = 61.7

2.15 Are the vibration frequencies given in Figure 2.13 consistent with equation (1) and the mode constants?

Some footbridges: their mode shapes and natural frequencies

Bridges can be made to vibrate, thus their natural frequencies and mode shapes may be found.

Figure 2.14 shows the result of mode and frequency tests on a footbridge in Scotland. The bridge is a continuous structure, a long steel box of rectangular cross-section with a steel deck. The central part, which is supported on piers, is 44 m long; the pedestrian deck is 2.5 m wide. The

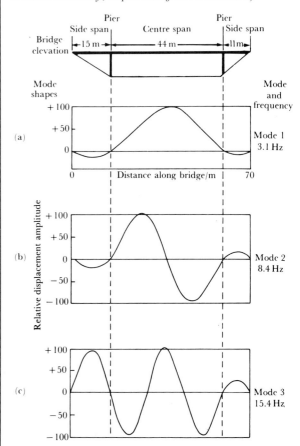

Figure 2.14 *An elevation diagram of the footbridge in Craigie Park, Ayr, Scotland. The bridge is of steel box construction. It is 70 m long and 2.5 m wide. Also shown are the first three mode shapes. (Source: Transport and Road Research Laboratory, Department of the Environment.)*

structure is therefore long compared with its width; and it can vibrate, very safely, with a motion that can be felt by pedestrians.

Figure 2.14(a)–(c) shows the first three vibration modes.

2.16 What are the first three natural vibration frequencies?

2.17 In the first vibration mode:
(a) Is a side span vibration in phase or out of phase with the centre span vibration?
(b) Are the vibrations of the side spans in phase with each other or out of phase?

(c) Sketch the vibration shape $\frac{1}{4}$ cycle after that shown in Figure 2.14(a). (The mode shape shows the *relative displacement amplitudes*.)

(d) Sketch the shape $\frac{1}{4}$ cycle after that shown in Figure 2.14(a).

(e) Is the mode shape in (a) completely symmetrical? If not, *where* is it not symmetrical; *why* is it not symmetrical?

(f) How many nodes are there?

(g) Where are the nodes, in terms of the bridge structure?

(h) Why are there nodes at these places?

2.18 In the second vibration mode:

(a) Are the side spans vibrating in phase or out of phase with each other?

(b) How many nodes are there?

2.19 In the third vibration mode:

(a) Which side span is vibrating with the greater amplitude?

(b) Why is this?

(c) What interesting feature do you notice about the amplitude of the left-hand side span and the amplitudes of the centre span sections?

(d) How might the situation in (c) come about? (Hint: look at the lengths of the side span and the centre span vibrating sections.)

Vibration experiments have been performed on the footbridge shown in Figure 2.15. The first experiments were conducted to find the natural frequencies and mode shapes. Later experiments were performed to find how rapidly vibrations built up when a pedestrian walked across the bridge, and how rapidly they died away. Further experiments were performed to determine whether the vibrations produced by pedestrians could be reduced in amplitude. (These later experiments are described in the sections on resonance and damping, pages 28–36.)

The basic structure of the Wharfe footbridge is shown in Figure 2.16. It is a steel box girder structure with a steel deck, shown in cross-section in (a). The centre span is a separate unit from the rest of the bridge. At each side of the river, a pier and cantilever were built; then the centre span, 32 m

Figure 2.15 *The footbridge over the River Wharfe at Wetherby, England, is a steel cantilever bridge with a suspended centre span. (Source: Transport and Road Research Laboratory, Department of the Environment.)*

Figure 2.16 *Diagrams of the footbridge in Figure 2.15, seen in cross-section and in elevation.*

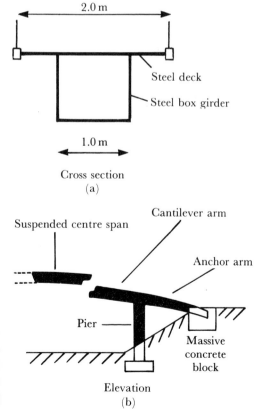

long, was lowered into position so that each end rested on the end of a cantilever arm. Each end of the centre span was then secured to its cantilever arm by means of steel pins.

2.20 Compare the photograph in Figure 2.15 with the elevation in Figure 2.16(b). In the photograph find (i) a pier; (ii) a massive concrete block (partly above ground level); (iii) the junction of a cantilever arm with the suspended centre span.

2.21 Describe briefly the function of the massive concrete block, using the term 'moment' in your description.

Figure 2.17 *An elevation drawing of the Wetherby footbridge (Figure 2.15); also shown are the first three vibration mode shapes.*

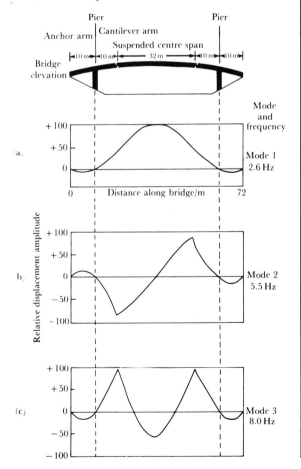

2.22 Study the elevation drawing in Figure 2.17. Is the bridge symmetrical?

2.23 What are the first three natural frequencies for the bridge?

2.24 Examine the first vibration mode shape:
(a) Where on the bridge would you stand in order to experience the maximum vibration?
(b) Does the bridge appear to be vibrating as a single continuous structure? (Are there any discontinuities in the mode shape?)
(c) Is the mode shape symmetrical?

2.25 Examine the second vibration mode shape:
(a) Where on the bridge would you stand in order to experience the maximum vibration?
(b) Does the bridge appear to be vibrating as a single continuous structure? (Are there any discontinuities in the mode shape?)
(c) If there are discontinuities, at what parts of the bridge do they occur?
(d) Why could they occur there?
(e) Sketch the relative position of the parts of the bridge a $\frac{1}{2}$ cycle later than the position shown in Figure 2.17(b). (The diagram shows the relative displacement amplitudes.)
(f) Are the anchor arms vibrating in phase or out of phase with each other?

Some vehicle mode shapes

Figure 2.18 shows an engine on its mountings, and the drive shaft to the rear axle. The rotations of the crankshaft and the drive shaft produce vibrations. The fixed points in the system, that is, mountings and the rear axle joint, cause nodes at those points. Any chosen point on the rest of the drive shaft moves in a circle and the vibration envelope has a circular cross-section.

In a vehicle, the rotation of the engine parts and the rotation of the drive shaft are sources of vibrations. When the frequency of one of these is the same as the natural frequency of another part of the vehicle, then that part of the vehicle will vibrate. In

Figure 2.18 *An engine and drive shaft producing a three-node drive line vibration. (Adapted from General Installation Handbook, Perkins Engines Limited.)*

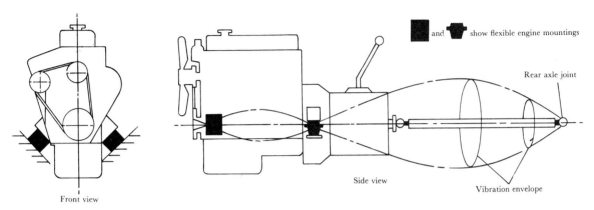

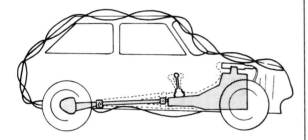

Figure 2.19 *A vibration pattern for the outer surface of a car. (Source: Bruel and Kjaer Limited.)*

Figure 2.19, the outer structure of the car has been set in vibration at one of its natural frequencies, and a pattern of nodes and antinodes results.

Machinery mounted on springs

Rotating machinery is often mounted on springs. The most frequent reason for this is to reduce the transmission of vibrations. If a large diesel engine is fixed directly to a floor, the vibrations of the engine will cause the floor to vibrate; and the floor vibrations could disturb other machinery or equipment. If the engine is mounted on springs, the transmission of vibrations to the floor can be reduced; that is, the springs help to isolate the vibrations of the engine.

In Figure 2.20, the springs will be used to

Figure 2.20 *Springs for supporting heavy vibrating machinery. (Source: Sound Attenuators Limited.)*

support heavy vibrating machinery. A common arrangement for this is seen in Figure 2.21, where a compressor and its electric motor are fixed to a steel base, which is supported on springs.

Figure 2.21 *Rotating machinery has been fixed to a steel base mounted on springs. (Source: Sound Attenuators Limited.)*

The reverse is also true: if floor vibrations could affect sensitive equipment, such as delicate instruments or microscopes, these can be mounted on springs. The springs then help to isolate the equipment from floor vibrations.

In either case, information about the *natural frequency of the system* that is on the springs is important. This is particularly true where rotating machinery is mounted on springs, because under certain conditions the vibrations can set the spring and mass system into violent and dangerous motion. This is considered in the section on resonance, pages 28–31.

Figure 2.22 shows the setting up of some machinery on to sprung bases. The diagrams are

elevation drawings and show two of the four springs that support the machinery. In (a) the springs are free and extended. In (b) a 400 kg base has been placed on the springs, which have been compressed. The depression of the top of each spring, caused by the weight of the base, is 2.5 mm. In an experiment, the base was forced down, further compressing the springs, and then suddenly released. The base vibrated freely up and down on the springs with a frequency of 10 Hz. Because the system was vibrating freely, it was vibrating at its *natural frequency*, which was thus 10 Hz.

In Figure 2.22(c), a machine of mass 200 kg has been placed on the base; the top of each spring has become further depressed, giving a total depression from their free positions in (a) of 3.75 mm. Forcing the machine and base down and then releasing them causes the system to vibrate up and down with a frequency of 8 Hz.

In Figure 2.22(d), the same type of springs and the same type of base, with a mass of 400 kg, is used to support a machine with a mass of 400 kg. The top of each spring is depressed from its free position by 5.0 mm. When forced down and suddenly released, the system vibrates at a frequency of 7 Hz.

2.26

(a) Do the springs obey Hooke's law?
(b) As the mass increases, does the vibration frequency increase or decrease?
(c) Does the relationship between the static depression and the system frequency appear to be linear or non-linear?

Figure 2.22 *An elevation drawing of springs and a base which are supporting machinery. The base is rectangular and is supported by four springs, one at each corner.*

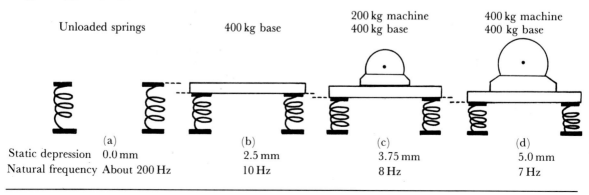

	Unloaded springs	400 kg base	200 kg machine 400 kg base	400 kg machine 400 kg base
	(a)	(b)	(c)	(d)
Static depression	0.0 mm	2.5 mm	3.75 mm	5.0 mm
Natural frequency	About 200 Hz	10 Hz	8 Hz	7 Hz

The first natural frequency of a vibrating system, the *fundamental frequency*, is given by the equation

$$f_0 = \frac{1}{2\pi} \sqrt{\left(\frac{k}{m}\right)} \qquad (2)$$

k = the stiffness of the spring
m = the mass of the system

Thus

$$f_0 \propto \sqrt{\left(\frac{1}{m}\right)} \quad \text{and} \quad f_0 \propto \sqrt{k}$$

The stiffness of the system is defined as the force which is required to produce unit deflection, 1 m. The SI units are newtons per metre, $N\,m^{-1}$.

For a soft spring, only a small force is needed to produce a deflection of 1 m. For a stiff spring, a large force is needed to produce a deflection of 1 m:

Stiffness $= k$

$$k = \frac{\text{Deflecting force}}{\text{Deflection produced}}; \text{ Units, } N\,m^{-1}$$

2.27

(a) For the sprung masses given in Figure 2.22, show that the vibration frequency is inversely proportional to $\sqrt{m}$. Use the data in Figure 2.22(b) and (d).

(b) From the data given in Figure 2.22(d), calculate the stiffness of one of the springs. (Four springs support the total load.)

(c) Use the spring stiffness which you have calculated in (b), and equation (2), to obtain the fundamental vibration frequency of the machine mounted on springs in Figure 2.22(d).

Some further calculations on sprung masses

2.28 Show that the equation for the fundamental frequency of vibration of a sprung mass is dimensionally correct, that is, equation (2) on page 27, where the stiffness of the spring is also defined.

Figure 2.23 A trailer on springs and solid wheels.

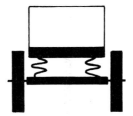

2.29 The trailer in Figure 2.23 has a body of mass 500 kg which is mounted on springs with a combined spring stiffness of $k = 60\,kN\,m^{-1}$. The wheels are solid. What is the vibration frequency of the body?

Figure 2.24 A trailer on inflexible mountings but with pneumatic rubber tyres.

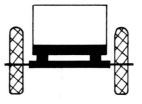

2.30 The trailer body illustrated in Figure 2.24 has a mass of 500 kg and is fixed to the chassis by inflexible mountings. The chassis has a mass of 400 kg and is attached to wheels which have pneumatic tyres. The combined stiffness of the tyres is $170\,kN\,m^{-1}$. What is the vibration frequency of the trailer on its tyres?

Figure 2.25 An aircraft mounted on trestles for testing.

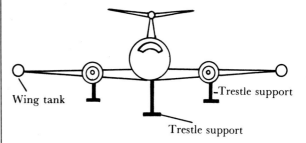

2.31 The aircraft shown in Figure 2.25 is almost at the final stage of construction and has been mounted on trestles for tests. One trestle has been placed under each engine. Each wingtip fuel tank has a mass of 200 kg, and the stiffness of a wing between the wingtip and the engine is 100 kN m^{-1}. Calculate the frequency of vertical vibrations which a wingtip tank and its outer wing section make about the fixed engine.

Figure 2.26 *The bridge beam is 26 m long and has a mass of 27 t.*

2.32 The bridge beam in Figure 2.26 is 26 m long. It was given a load and deflection test by the manufacturer, as follows. The beam was supported at each end on rigid supports. A load equivalent to 47 t was then placed at the centre of the beam, and a deflection of the beam centre of 47 mm occurred.
(a) What is the stiffness, k, of the beam?
(b) What is the vibration frequency of the unloaded beam in its fundamental mode? (Use equation (2) to obtain an approximate value. The actual situation is complex.)

2.33 A rectangular panel made of thin sheet steel is vibrating at a frequency of 1000 Hz and is causing annoyance. An attempt to reduce the vibration is made by painting a mastic material onto the panel. The sheet steel panel has a mass of 0.90 kg, and when the mastic has been spread on the surface the total mass of steel and mastic is 1.80 kg. Assume that the stiffness of the painted panel is the same as the stiffness of the original sheet. Calculate the vibration frequency of the painted panel.

Resonance

In 1850 a battalion of French infantrymen marched in step across the suspension bridge at Angers. As they did so, the bridge began to oscillate. The men continued to march and the displacement amplitude of the oscillation grew greater and greater until the bridge materials could no longer stand the strain and the bridge collapsed. The 500 men dropped into a ravine and 226 of them were killed.

The frequency of the soldiers' tramping feet was the same as the natural vibration frequency of the bridge. Men march at about 120 steps per minute, which is a frequency of 2 steps per second, or 2 Hz. A very common natural vibration frequency for a bridge is about 2 Hz.

At regular intervals of twice every second, 500 feet came down on the bridge, feeding energy into it. The feet arriving on the deck and the motion of the deck were synchronised; thus every new pulse of energy from the feet forced the bridge into greater motion.

Resonance had occurred in the bridge.

For resonance to occur, three conditions are needed. There must be *a system which can vibrate* (such as the bridge); there must be *a supply of energy in pulses*; and the energy pulses must be fed into the system at *the natural vibration frequency of the system*. That is, the energy pulse frequency must be the same as the system's natural vibration frequency.

The *incoming energy* becomes *stored in the vibrations* of the system: as *kinetic energy* in the moving masses, and as *potential energy* in the elastic strain in the structure.

Figure 2.27 shows a heavy machine on a factory floor. When running, the machine rotates and imparts upward and downward forces on the floor, causing the floor and machine to move up and down.

Figure 2.27(a) shows the machine stationary, its weight causing the floor to sag slightly. If the machine and floor were forced down and then suddenly released they would vibrate up and down as a unit at 10 Hz, the natural frequency of the floor and machine combination.

The machine is then started and its rotation speed is slowly increased. In Figure 2.27(b), at 180 rev min^{-1} or 3 Hz, small vertical vibrations result. As the speed is increased through 300 rev min^{-1} (5 Hz), 420 rev min^{-1} (7 Hz), and so on, the

Figure 2.27 *A factory floor with a heavy rotating machine on it. The natural vertical vibration frequency of the floor with the machine on it is 10 Hz.*

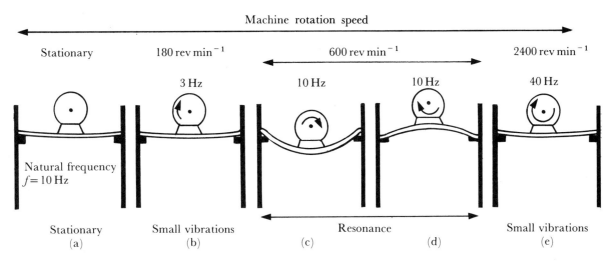

vibrations remain small. But suddenly, at 600 rev min^{-1} (10 Hz), the vertical movements of the floor and machine increase greatly. This is shown in Figure 2.27(c) and (d). The system has gone into resonance; the forcing frequency from the machine has become equal to the natural frequency of the system. More energy is being stored in every successive vibration, and the displacement amplitude is increasing. A point could be reached where the floor becomes unable to stand the strain imposed on it and it breaks, allowing the machine and disintegrated floor to drop down onto the floor below. This has happened in first-floor workshops.

When the rotation speed is increased to over 600 rev min^{-1} (over 10 Hz) the system goes out of resonance. The vibrations of the floor and machine combination become small again. Figure 2.27(e) shows the situation at 2400 rev min^{-1} (40 Hz), and although the rotation speed is high the vibration amplitude is small.

2.34 Figure 2.28 shows a rotating machine on the first floor of a building. The natural vibration frequencies of an office floor, a ceiling, and two windows are marked on the drawing. The operator at the control panel starts the machine and slowly increases its speed to 4000 rev min^{-1}. Describe what might be felt and heard in the building during this run up to 4000 rev min^{-1}.

Figure 2.28 *A building with a rotating machine on the first floor. The natural vibration frequencies of four parts of the building are given. Vibrations in one part of a building can travel along the floors and up and down the walls, and can cause other parts of the building to vibrate.*

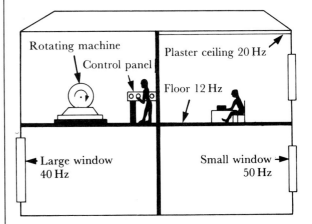

Every structure and machine can be made to vibrate, and a complex structure or machine will have *several* natural frequencies. If it is caused to vibrate at any of these frequencies then resonance will occur; vibrations of great amplitude may build up and the structure or machine may break up.

Bridges, internal combustion engines, electric motors, turbine blades, propulsion shafts, fans, aircraft wings, and all other structures, have to be studied at the design stage to determine as closely as possible what their natural frequencies are likely to be. Exciting forces at these frequencies must then be avoided; if this is not possible the design will have to be changed and a natural vibration will need to be moved to a different frequency value.

Figure 2.29 *(a) Some of the main natural vibration frequencies of a vehicle. (b) The most commonly used engine speeds coincide with two of the natural frequencies. (Modified from a diagram of Dunlop Limited, Polymer Engineering Division.)*

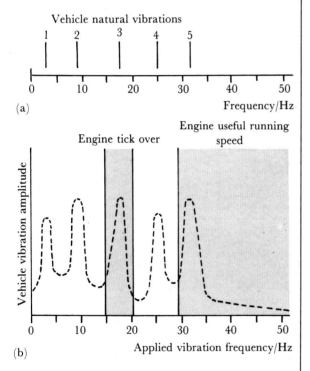

(a)

(b)

Figure 2.29(a) shows five of the natural vibration frequencies of a prototype vehicle: at about 3 Hz, 8 Hz, 17 Hz, 25 Hz and 32 Hz.

If the vehicle is placed in a test rig and vibrated at increasing vibration frequencies, 1 Hz, 2 Hz, 3 Hz, the vibration amplitude of the vehicle will suddenly rise at about 3 Hz, the vibrations perhaps becoming quite violent. With an input vibratory force at a frequency of 3 Hz, the 3 Hz natural vibration frequency has been excited and resonance is occurring. On increasing the frequency of the exciting force to 4 Hz and 5 Hz the vibration

amplitude of the vehicle will drop. This is shown in Figure 2.29(b). A peak in the vehicle vibration amplitude occurs at 3 Hz. As the frequency of the applied vibration is increased, so further natural frequencies are excited and further resonances occur.

Under normal running conditions, the rotating engine would provide the alternating force which would vibrate the vehicle as a whole. On starting the engine, the revolutions rapidly increase from 0 to about 15–20 rev s^{-1}. They pass so rapidly through the first two natural frequencies that the system does not have time to go into resonance. The engine then runs at tickover speed. This could be around 15–20 rev s^{-1}. The tickover speed might be about 18 rev s^{-1}, in which case it would excite the third natural frequency of 18 Hz and resonance would occur.

A similar problem would occur when the car was being driven along and the engine running speed was about 32 rev s^{-1}. Then the fifth natural frequency would be excited and vibrations of large amplitude would build up rapidly.

Natural vibration frequencies cannot be allowed to exist within the frequency range of an exciting force. The prototype vehicle therefore has to be modified. The design has to be altered so that the

Figure 2.30 *The natural vibration frequencies for a modified design of the vehicle. The natural frequencies fall outside the main running speeds of the engine. (Modified from a diagram of Dunlop Limited, Polymer Engineering Division.)*

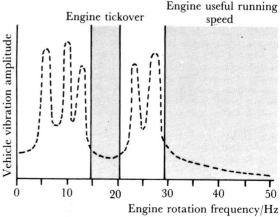

natural frequencies lie outside the forcing frequencies. Figure 2.30 shows an acceptable pattern, obtained by modifying the prototype vehicle.

2.35 Compare Figure 2.30 with Figure 2.29. Describe simply what has happened to the natural frequencies that were unacceptable.

2.36 Are the other natural frequencies the same as before? Suggest a likely reason for what you observe.

Damping

If the amplitude of a natural vibration is to be reduced, then energy must be removed from the vibrating system. Reducing the amplitude of a vibration by removing energy from it is known as *damping*.

In mechanical vibrations the most common means by which energy is removed from the system is through *friction*. The moving parts of the system experience friction forces: solid over solid; solid over lubricating fluid; solid structure moving through air; and solid structure moving through fluid. The result of movement against a friction force is heat; kinetic energy from the vibrating system is changed into heat.

In free vibrations, where after the initial input of energy there is no further input of energy, the loss of energy through movement against friction forces will gradually stop the vibrations.

Friction damping will oppose existing vibrations, and will reduce their amplitude.
Friction damping will oppose new vibrations, and will result in smaller new amplitudes than if less friction were present.

Figure 2.31 shows two vibration traces for the footbridge across the River Wharfe at Wetherby in England. A photograph of the bridge is shown in Figure 2.15 on page 23. Its cantilever structure and suspended centre span are shown in Figure 2.16 on page 23 and in Figure 2.17 on page 24. Look again at these three diagrams.

Modern footbridges are designed to be safe even if a pedestrian strides across at paces which are at the natural frequency of the bridge. The bridge may feel 'lively', but it will be safe.

The trace shown in Figure 2.31(a) shows the displacement amplitude of the centre of the bridge, in millimetres, against time, in seconds, as a pedestrian paced across at the bridge's natural frequency. The person strode onto the bridge at the end of an anchor arm at time $t = 0$ s, was at the middle of the bridge at time $t = 11$ s (approx.), and stepped off the bridge at the other bank at time $t = 22$ s (approx.).

2.37 From the trace, work out the natural vibration frequency of the bridge. On the basis of your knowledge of typical natural frequencies for bridges, does your value seem to be reasonable?

2.38 What was the maximum amplitude reached?

2.39 Was this maximum amplitude reached when the person was at the centre of the bridge or after the centre?

2.40 Account for what you find in Question 2.39.
As the person walks along the anchor arm and onto the bank, the vibrations of the centre of the bridge continue. They decay slowly.

The trace shown in Figure 2.31(b), gives the vibrations which were recorded with the same excitation, that is, the same person pacing across the bridge in the same manner, but with a damper fitted to the bridge. The damper consisted of a piston in a container of oil; as the bridge moved, so the piston moved up and down in the oil. In moving the piston, the bridge worked against the force of friction in the viscous oil, and energy was removed from the bridge. In the process, the temperature of the oil rose and energy transfer to the atmosphere resulted, in the form of heat.

The overall change was therefore a loss of kinetic energy by the bridge, and an equivalent heat transfer to the atmosphere.

Examine Figure 2.31(b), which is the vibration trace for the bridge with the damper attached; compare it with the trace for the undamped bridge, trace (a).

2.41 Estimate the maximum displacement amplitude reached by the damped bridge.

2.42 Express this as a fraction of the maximum for the undamped bridge.

Figure 2.31 *Vibration traces for a footbridge when a pedestrian walked smartly across it, pacing at the natural vibration frequency of the footbridge: (a) the upper curve is for the bridge without any attachments; (b) the lower curve is for the bridge with a damper attached. (Source: Dr A. J. Pretlove, Journal of the Institution of Structural Engineers, 1981.)*

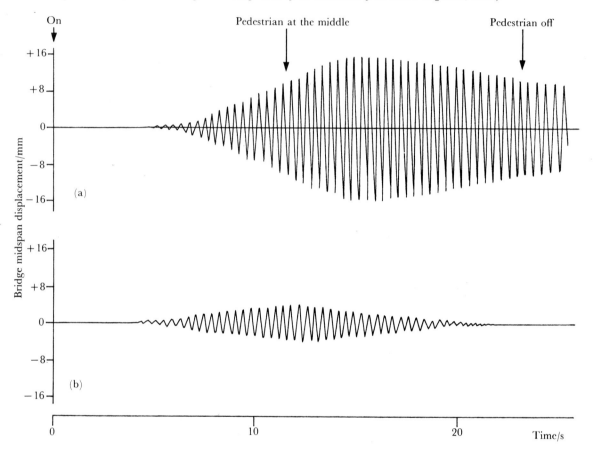

2.43 Did the vibrations die down faster when the damper was in use?

2.44 Had the vibrations of the centre of the damped bridge died down (for practical purposes) by the time the pedestrian stepped off the anchor arm?

2.45 Compare this with the situation for the undamped bridge.

2.46 Find the time at which the maximum vibration occurred in the damped bridge. Was it the same as for the undamped bridge?

2.47 Suggest the reason for what you find.

The damper for this bridge was a piston, moving in an oil bath and placed at the midspan of the bridge. The dynamics of this damper are not simple and we need not examine them here. The essential feature was that the movement of a piston in a cylinder containing oil resulted in *energy being removed from the system*, through *friction between the piston and the oil*, and subsequent *heat transfer*.

Energy removed by a damper

Figure 2.32 shows an elevation drawing of a footbridge across a motorway. The main span is 57 m long, and the whole bridge is made of light,

Figure 2.32 *Elevation drawing and cross-section of the footbridge over the M5 motorway at Clapton-in-Gordano, Avon, England. The bridge is a slender steel box and could be 'lively' with pedestrians on it. A friction damper was fitted. (Source: Transport and Road Research Laboratory, Department of the Environment; Dr T. Wyatt.)*

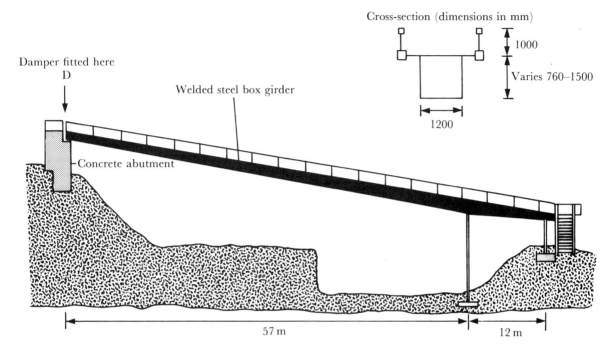

steel boxes welded together. The designers realised at the design stage that the bridge would vibrate appreciably and would feel 'lively' to pedestrians walking over it. The amount of damping that would be needed was difficult to predict, so it was decided to build the bridge, test its vibration characteristics, and then calculate the amount of damping that was needed. A suitable damper could then be designed and fitted.

After the bridge had been built and tested, discussions were held and the decision taken to make a sliding friction damper, and to place it in the expansion and contraction joint between the upper end of the box girder and the abutment. This is marked D on the left-hand side of Figure 2.32.

Figure 2.33 is a plan drawing of the damper which was fixed in one handrail of the bridge, at position D in Figure 2.32. As the centre of the box girder moved up and down, the end at D moved in and out, towards and away from the abutment. The left-hand part of the damper in Figure 2.33

was fixed to the abutment and thus remained stationary at all times.

2.48 Describe briefly how the damper removes energy from the vibrating bridge.

2.49 When the amplitude of up and down vibrations at the centre of the long span is 15 mm, the end of the span at D moves towards and away from the abutment with an amplitude of 1.2 mm. Thus, at this amplitude the brake linings move against the steel of the handrails.

The friction force which opposes motion at each brake lining is 1500 N.

The vibration frequency is 2 Hz:
(a) In one cycle, what total distance does a brake lining move?
(b) In one cycle how much work is done against friction by one brake lining?
(c) In one cycle, how much energy is removed from the vibrating bridge by one brake lining?

Figure 2.33 *A plan view (approximately ½ size) of the friction damper that was designed for the bridge. A single damper consists of two brake linings sliding against the insides of one of the steel hand rails. (Source: Transport and Road Research Laboratory, Department of the Environment; Dr T. Wyatt.)*

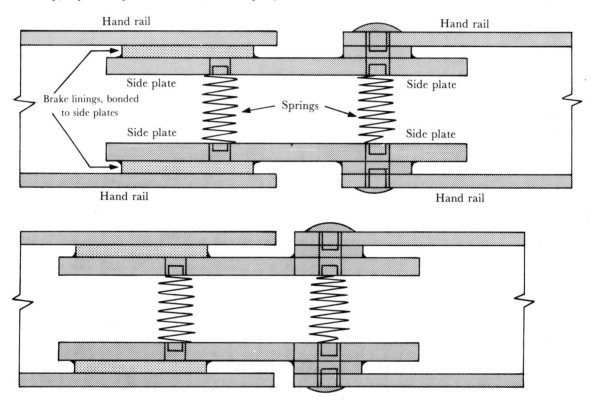

(d) What is the power removed from the bridge vibrations by one brake lining?
   (Power = energy transfer per second.)

(e) The complete damping system has four brake linings (two handrails, and two linings in each handrail). What is the total power removed from the vibrating bridge by the complete damping system?

2.50 When the amplitude of vertical movements at the centre of the long span is 40 mm, the amplitude of the brake lining motion in the dampers is 3.4 mm. What is the power being removed from the vibrating bridge by the dampers?

A friction damper for spring-mounted machinery

Rotating machinery is mounted in such a way that the transmission of vibrations is reduced as much as possible. The machinery is frequently mounted on springs. The behaviour of rotating machinery mounted on springs was described in pages 25–27 and you should look back to this, particularly Figures 2.20, 2.21, and 2.22.

Here, Figure 2.34 shows rotating machinery. At the far left is a diesel engine which is driving an alternator (near right) to produce alternating current. Both are mounted on a steel frame. The steel frame is on spring mountings (the springs are concealed by the outer covers). The natural frequencies of systems such as these lie between about 2.5 Hz and 6 Hz.

Figure 2.34 *Rotating machinery, on a steel frame base, mounted on spring supports with friction dampers. (Source: Barry Controls Limited.)*

When the engine is started, the revolution speed begins at zero, increases and reaches the natural frequency of the system somewhere around 2.5 Hz–6 Hz, and the system begins to go into resonance. If vibration energy can be removed, resonance can be controlled. Figure 2.35 shows the friction damper used for the spring mountings in the photograph in Figure 2.34.

Examine the drawing of the spring support and friction damper in Figure 2.35. Work out the function of each labelled part.

2.51 Which parts move?

2.52 Which parts remain stationary?

2.53 Where does the energy transformation, which removes energy from the vibrations, take place?

Figure 2.35 *The spring support and friction damper for the mountings in Figure 2.34. (Adapted from a drawing of Barry Controls Limited.)*

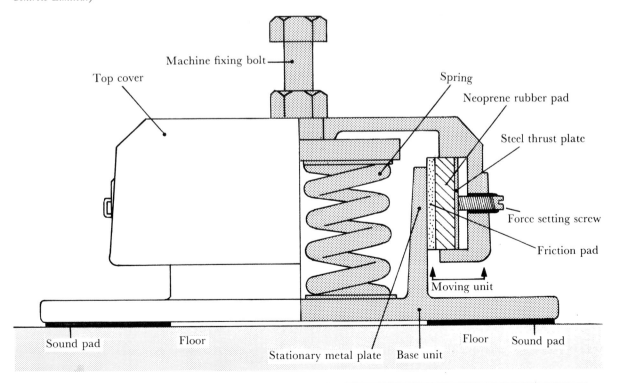

2.54 Describe (a) the energy transformation, and (b) the routes by which the transformed energy escapes from the system.

2.55 Suggest a reason why the designers included
(a) a Neoprene rubber pad;
(b) a force setting screw.

Controlling systems which are in resonance

If a system goes into resonance and its amplitude continues to increase, the basic way to control it is to remove energy from the system.

Sometimes the natural energy loss, usually as heat, rises until the energy input and energy loss equal each other; then the system remains at a fixed amplitude. If this does not happen before an undesirably large or dangerous amplitude is reached, then energy must be removed by special means; that is, damping must be used.

Answers to text questions

2.3 (a) 53.3 Hz; (b) 1342 Hz; (d) 1575 Hz, 1575 Hz, 1692 Hz.

2.8 About $1\,\mathrm{m\,s^{-1}}$ to $3\,\mathrm{m\,s^{-2}}$.

2.12 10 pC.

2.13 $2.5\,\mathrm{m\,s^{-2}}$.

2.27 (b) $1.6 \times 10^6\,\mathrm{N\,m^{-1}}$; (c) 7.1 Hz.

2.29 1.7 Hz.

2.30 2.2 Hz.

2.31 3.6 Hz.

2.32 (a) $10\,\mathrm{MN\,m^{-1}}$; (b) 3.1 Hz.

2.33 707 Hz.

2.37 2.5 Hz or 2.6 Hz.

2.38 15 mm or 16 mm.

2.41 4 mm or 5 mm.

2.42 About $\frac{1}{4}$.

2.49 (a) 4.8 mm; (b) 7.2 J; (c) 7.2 J; (d) 14 W; (e) 58 W.

2.50 160 W.

3. Circular motion 1: unbalanced machinery

The forces which are produced in rotating machinery are of great importance in engineering. They lead to strain in machinery, and they are a major cause of vibrations.

If a mass m is rotating with an angular velocity of ω, and if the centre of mass is at a distance r from the centre of rotation, then the force F which is needed to keep the mass in circular motion is $F = m\omega^2 r$. The force acts through the centre of mass and towards the centre of rotation.

Figure 3.1 A cam-shaped mass fixed to an axle. The axle is mounted on two supports and can rotate in these; m indicates the centre of mass of the cam. (This diagram may be photocopied.)

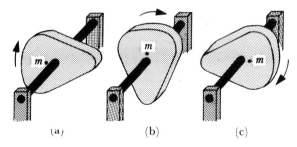

(a)   (b)   (c)

The cam-shaped mass in Figure 3.1 is rotating in a clockwise direction on an axle which is free to move in two vertical supports.

3.1 Use a copy of Figure 3.1 for the following exercise.

(a) On your copy of Figure 3.1(a) draw a line with an arrow which represents the direction of the force on the cam, keeping it in circular motion.

(b) Draw the length of the arrow to represent the magnitude of the force.

(c) Visualise the direction of the force when the cam has rotated through $90°$, as is shown in Figure 3.1(b). On your copy of Figure 3.1(b) mark an arrow to show the force which is experienced by the *axle* where it passes through the cam. Use an arrow to show the direction and magnitude of the force.

(d) Similarly, visualise the forces in Figure 3.1(c). Now visualise the force at each *vertical support*, due to the rotation of the cam. On your copy, draw arrows on each vertical support to represent the force due to the rotation. Draw the arrows to represent the forces in direction and magnitude.

(e) Sketch a vertical support and a fourth position, (d), for the cam. At the support draw an arrow to represent the force on it due to the rotation.

(f) Sketch another supporting post under each position (a), (b), (c) and (d). Mark at each post the direction of the force on the post, due to rotation.

(g) Describe in a simple manner the effect which the rotation is having on the support. Then give a single word which summarises the effect.

Unbalance in rotating machinery

It is almost impossible to produce a rotating machine that is perfectly balanced. If the machine is not balanced, then rotation of the off-the-axis centre of mass produces a cyclic force on the supports; and the supports vibrate.

Unbalance is a major source of vibration in all types of machinery which have rotating parts; examples are engine flywheels, clutch plates, brake discs, vehicle wheels, gear wheels, spin driers in domestic washing machines, centrifuges, coil groups in electric motors, coil groups in alternators for producing alternating current, rotating shafts, engine crankshafts, and turbine wheels. One cause of unbalance is asymmetry in the shape of rotating components such as in a cam on a camshaft (Figure 3.1), or in an engine crankshaft (Figure 3.8). Another source lies in the complexities of manufacturing processes; even a component whose design shape is symmetrical can prove to be unbalanced.

Figure 3.2 *Two flywheels. In (a) the axle is central but two cavities cause the centre of mass, M, to be off the axis. In (b) the centre of mass is at the geometrical centre but the axle is off-centre. Both give unbalanced rotors and lead to vibrations.*

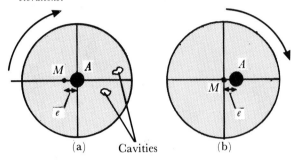

(a)   Cavities   (b)

In Figure 3.2 are two flywheels, each of which is unbalanced. In (a), blowholes in the casting have produced two cavities and have shifted the centre of mass off the axis; in (b), the axle has been mounted off the geometrical centre of the wheel. In each case, rotation will produce a cyclic force on the supports and will lead to vibration. The distance of the centre of mass from the axis of rotation is shown as e, the eccentricity.

A part that has to be machined to the correct size and shape may have had slightly too much metal machined off one side. A heat treatment process can lead to slight distortion of shape.

If the rotation speed is high, very small errors in the distribution of mass can lead to large cyclic forces and thus to large vibrations.

3.2 A flywheel of mass 1 t rotates at 500 rev min^{-1} and is found to produce a maximum horizontal force of 300 N on each of the axle bearings (two bearings, one for each end of the axle).
   (a) What is the centripetal force exerted by the axle on the rotating mass?
   (b) Using the relationship $F = m\omega^2 e$, what is the eccentricity?

From the calculations it is seen that an eccentricity of less than 1 mm is causing cyclic forces on the supports equal to the weight of a 30 kg mass. A small eccentricity can lead to large forces and thus to large vibrations. National standards have been developed for the eccentricities of different types of rotating machinery, to ensure that they lie within an acceptable limit. One standard used by many nations is given in Table 3.1.

Table 3.1. *Some machine speeds, and allowable eccentricities.*

Type of rotating machine	Typical service speed (rev min^{-1})	Allowable eccentricity (μm)
Vehicle engine crankshafts	6 000	60
Large electric motors	1 500	40
Precision electric motors	6 000	1.6
Reference gyroscopes	24 000	0.15

Thus, reference gyroscopes have to be made with very great precision and balance, and have an eccentricity of less than 1 μm. Even a vehicle engine crankshaft has to be manufactured so that its eccentricity is less than 0.1 mm.

Machining a part until its balance is acceptable can be very expensive. A more common procedure is to add counterbalancing masses, or to drill out some mass.

Balancing unbalanced rotors: counterbalances

One of the most common ways of rectifying unbalance in a rotor is by adding a counterbalancing mass. In Figure 3.3 the centre of mass, M, of the flywheel is eccentric to the axis of rotation, A, by a distance e. This can be remedied by placing a counterbalancing mass, m, on the diameter joining M and A, with m and M being on opposite sides of the axis of rotation.

The centripetal force required to keep M in rotation and that required to keep m in rotation

Figure 3.3 *A flywheel of mass M. The centre of mass is eccentric from the axis of rotation, A, by a distance e. A small mass, m, has been fixed as a counterbalance.*

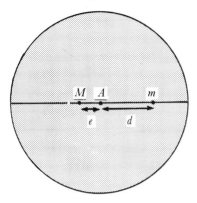

Figure 3.4 *The fan is being adjusted for balance. Rivets are being fixed near the edge of a blade to add mass. (Source: Schenck Limited.)*

must be opposite in direction, and their sum must be zero. Therefore

$$M\omega^2 e + (-m\omega^2 d) = 0$$
$$M\omega^2 e = m\omega^2 d$$

and

$$Me = md$$

3.3 Consider again the 1 t flywheel in Question 3.2. A counterbalancing mass is to be placed a distance of 1 m from the axis of rotation. What should be the value of the mass? (The eccentricity, e, of the flywheel was calculated in Question 3.2.)

Figures 3.4 and 3.5 show rotating components being adjusted because of unbalance. In Figure 3.4, counterbalancing of a vehicle engine fan is being carried out by adding extra mass to one fan blade, in the form of rivets near one edge. Figure 3.5 shows the rotor coils for an alternator to generate alternating current. Alternator rotor coils have to rotate at high speed, typically 3000 rev min^{-1}, and the unbalance must be very low. In Figure 3.5, metal is being removed from one of the coil supports by drilling a hole in the metal of the support.

In an internal combusion engine, the piston has to be connected to a crank in order to produce rotary motion in a shaft. Figure 3.6 shows a very simple crank.

Examine Figure 3.6 and find which masses rotate as the piston moves down and then up, and

down again. What effect will this have on the *crankshaft*? The masses of the crank pin, the crank, and the big end of the connecting rod form an unbalanced mass on the crankshaft as an axle. In order to keep this mass in motion around the shaft, a centripetal force, F_C, has to be applied to it. This force produces an equal and opposite reaction force, F_R, on the shaft. As common rotation speeds for petrol and diesel engines lie between 2000 rev min^{-1} and 3600 rev min^{-1}, the centripetal force and the reaction on the shaft could be very large and could lead to serious strains and vibrations. The unbalanced masses thus have to be balanced as far as possible, within the limits usually set by cost.

Figure 3.7 shows a crank which is an improvement on that shown in Figure 3.6; it has a counterbalancing mass. If the balancing is correct, the centripetal force required to keep the counterbalancing mass in circular motion will be *equal in magnitude* and *opposite in direction* to the centripetal

Figure 3.5 *The rotor coils of an alternator being adjusted for balance. Metal is being drilled out of a coil support to reduce mass. (Source: Schenck Limited.)*

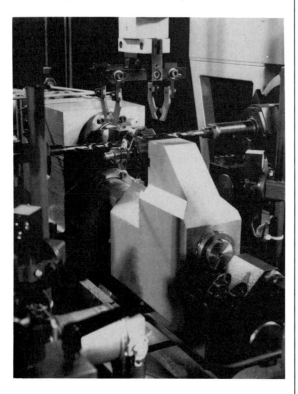

Figure 3.6 *The piston of an unbalanced engine, and the parts which connect the piston to the crankshaft. The big end of the connecting rod, the crank pin and the crank form an unbalanced rotating mass.*

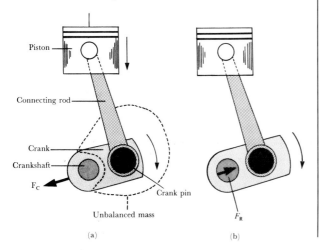

Piston

Connecting rod

Crank

Crankshaft

F_C

Crank pin

Unbalanced mass

(a)

F_R

(b)

Figure 3.7 *A crank, with a counterbalancing mass on the opposite side of the shaft to the crank pin.*

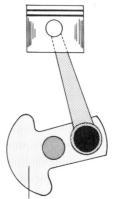

Counterbalancing mass

force required to keep the crank pin, its end of the crank and the lower part of the connecting rod in circular motion.

It is very expensive to achieve near-perfect balance, and in practice balancing is done until unbalance and its associated vibrations have been reduced to an acceptably low level.

In order to know whether a rotor is balanced or not, it is necessary to test it. Figure 3.8 shows a

Figure 3.8 *A machine for measuring the unbalance of rotors. The crankshaft of a small, four-cylinder engine is mounted for testing on the two white pillars. At the left-hand side is an electric motor which rotates the rotor. Vibration levels are measured by accelerometers in the vertical supports near the bearings. (The accelerometers are not visible.) The overall length of the base is about 1 m. (Source: Bruel and Kjaer Limited.)*

balance testing machine. The amount of unbalance in the rotor is determined by measuring the vibration level at the supports. For this purpose an accelerometer is mounted in each support.

Figure 3.8 also shows a crankshaft for a small four-cylinder engine mounted on the supports. The crankshaft will be driven round by the electric motor at the left of the assembly.

3.4 Examine the crankshaft in Figure 3.8.
  (a) Find four counterbalancing masses.
  (b) Find the axis of the crankshaft (lay a ruler along the crankshaft and the electric motor driveline).
  (c) Find four positions at which the big end of a connecting rod will be attached.
  (d) Is each of these positions approximately opposite a counterbalancing mass?

By measuring the accelerations produced at each support by the forces from unbalanced rotation, it is possible to calculate where the unbalance is and hence how to correct it.

In Figure 3.9 two cam-shaped masses are fixed on an axle in diametrically opposite directions to each other. When stationary, they are in balance. If the system is turned to a particular position and then left, it remains in that position. If the axle is rotated steadily, however, causing the two masses to rotate with it, the supports experience out-of-balance forces, and the supporting structure vibrates. There are two types of balance: *static balance* and *dynamic balance*.

Figure 3.9 *The two cam-shaped masses are fixed to an axle. When the axle and its masses are stationary they are balanced. When they are rotating, they are unbalanced. Why? (This figure may be photocopied.)*

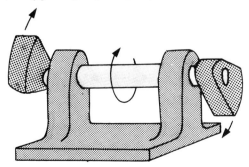

3.5 Examine Figure 3.9 and consider how it can be statically balanced and yet dynamically unbalanced
  (a) For the left-hand mass, mark the approximate centre of the mass. Through it draw an arrow vertically downwards to represent the force due to the weight of the mass and label it W_1. Draw a line from the centre of mass to meet the axis of rotation at right-angles and label it length d_1.
  (b) What effect is weight W_1 having on the system?
  (c) Repeat for the right-hand mass.
  (d) What effect is the weight, W_2, of the second mass having on the system?
  (e) Using the word 'moments', describe the effect which leads to static balance.
  (f) Will this situation be so for all positions of the two masses?
  (g) Now consider the system when it is rotating. Near the left-hand end of the axle, draw in the direction of a reaction force on the axle due to the rotation of the mass; label it FR_1.
  (h) Repeat for the right-hand mass; label the reaction force FR_2.
  (i) Using the word 'couple', describe what is happening. Does the situation lead to balance or to unbalance?

Measurements of vibrations at two supports enable the *magnitude* and *direction* of unbalance to be found. The direction would be in relation to some part of the rotating equipment, for instance the line of one of the cranks. The equipment can then be balanced by adding masses, usually in two or more different planes, to give both static balance and dynamic balance. All crankshafts are tested in this way during manufacture, and are adjusted for balance.

A case history: vibrations in a gantry crane

Figure 3.10 shows a gantry crane in a shipbuilding works. Such a crane is mounted on sets of wheels on rails and is able to move along the length of the

Figure 3.10 *A large gantry crane in a shipbuilding works. When the crane was operating, very heavy vibrations were occurring in the whole of the gantry structure. (Source: Bruel and Kjaer Limited.)*

dock. A winch is mounted on the cross-beam of the crane; the winch is mounted on rollers and can be moved along the cross-beam, that is, sideways across the dock. In these ways the winch can be positioned above any point of a ship under construction.

After the crane had given good service over a long period, heavy vibrations suddenly developed. These shook the whole gantry structure. The production management was in a dilemma. Dismantling the winch and motor units to look for the cause would involve a production stoppage, and that would be very costly. On the other hand, to do nothing would almost certainly lead to a complete breakdown, and that would be even more expensive.

Preliminary investigations showed that the vibrations were only present when a particular winch unit was being used to hoist a load. Vibration measurements on the winch showed that the source was in the gear box.

Vibration measurements were made on the gearbox of the crane, and Figure 3.11 shows this operation. The vibrations were measured at a succession of different frequencies, from about 1 Hz to about 50 Hz; at each frequency the magnitude of the vibrations was found. Figure 3.12 gives the results.

The most violent vibrations were found to be at 11 Hz. In this case, the rotation speed of the intermediate gear was known to be 660 rev min^{-1}, which is 11 Hz. Thus the intermediate gear was the source of the vibrations.

Figure 3.11 *Vibration measurements being made on the winch gearbox of the crane. (Source: Bruel and Kjaer Limited.)*

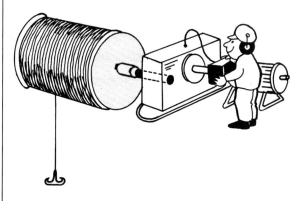

Figure 3.12 *Results of vibration measurements on the winch gearbox. The measurements were made at frequencies from about 1 Hz to about 50 Hz. The graph shows the magnitude of the vibrations at different frequencies. (Source: Bruel and Kjaer LImited.)*

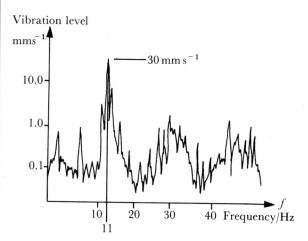

From the vibration measurements, the centripetal force due to unbalance in the rotating gear wheel was found to be 8290 N. Now

$$F_{\text{unbalance}} = mr\omega^2 = mr(2\pi f)^2$$

where m is the unbalance mass, r is the distance of its centre of mass from the axis of rotation, ω is angular velocity, and f is the frequency of rotation.

3.6 Using the data which has been given for the unbalance force and for the vibration frequency, find the value of the product (mr).

Figure 3.13 *When the gearbox was opened and the gear wheel inspected, a piece of metal with a mass of 3.3 kg was found to have broken off the wheel. (Source: Bruel and Kjaer Limited.)*

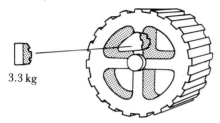

3.3 kg

At some convenient time when the winch was not in use, the gearbox was opened and the intermediate gear wheel was inspected. A piece of metal with a mass of 3.3 kg had broken off the gear wheel. This is shown in Figure 3.13. When the piece was fixed in position, its centre of mass was 0.53 m from the axis of rotation.

3.7 Use the measurements which were obtained on opening the gearbox, and obtain a value for the product (mr).

3.8 How does the result obtained from direct inspection compare with the result obtained indirectly from vibration measurements? (The latter was calculated in question 3.6.)

Advantages of good balancing of rotating machinery

If rotating machinery is badly out of balance, large cyclic forces may develop and may lead to break-up of part of the assembled product. Even if the machinery were not so out of balance as the extreme situation just mentioned, considerable advantages can be gained by balancing the rotor as efficiently as the economics of the situation will allow.

If the rotor is well balanced, the advantages for the assembled final machinery are

- reduced wear on bearings;
- reduced likelihood of loosening of fastenings (through reduced vibration);
- reduced likelihood of fatigue failure of bracket supports and of housings (through reduced vibrations);
- reduced transmission of vibrations to the building's foundations and thus to any other machinery in it;
- reduced noise (through reduced vibrations);
- lengthened product life.

A rotor which is balanced at the beginning of its service may in the course of long use go out of balance. Two causes of this are uneven wear on the rotor and corrosion of the rotor, each of which alters the mass. Another cause is growing distortion of the rotor due to misalignment of the machinery when it was assembled. Because of these and other effects, a rotor may have to be rebalanced, perhaps several times, during its lifetime.

Answers to text questions

3.2 (a) 600 N; (b) 0.2 mm.
3.3 0.2 kg.
3.5 (j) Yes.
3.6 1.73 kg m, or 1.74 kg m.
3.7 1.75 kg m.

4. Circular motion 2: an automatic centripetal brake

Figure 4.1 *The outer part and the inner rotating part of an automatic brake. It is used for braking rotating machinery. The outer case measures about $\frac{1}{4}$ m across.*

The photograph in Figure 4.1 shows an industrial automatic brake which is used to prevent a shaft from rotating too fast.

The manufacturer's information leaflet states:

These particular units are normally used for emergency purposes only. They are designed to prevent a shaft from rotating too fast, for instance when a lifeboat is being lowered, or in the descent of a lift, or in the lowering of a load on a crane.

The inner part of the brake unit is fitted to the shaft, and at normal rotation speeds the brake shoes are retracted and do not touch the outer cover.

The manufacturer's notes give a brief account of the operation of the brake. Refer to Figures 4.1 and 4.2 in reading the notes, and locate the main parts of the brake, which are underlined.

The working parts consist of a <u>stationary outer unit</u>, and an <u>inner rotating unit</u> which is in the <u>form of four arms</u>. Between adjacent arms is a <u>brake shoe</u>, which is held in place by a spiral spring that is set to provide a predetermined restraining force. When the shaft is lifting a load and is rotating slowly, the inner brake unit rotates slowly and the shoes are held in place by their springs. When the shaft is lowering a load at a higher but still safe speed, the shoes remain held in position by their springs.

If the lowering speed increases and approaches an unsafe value, the preset restraining force of the spiral

Figure 4.2 *Two sections of the automatic brake. They are approximately $\frac{1}{3}$ actual size. (This figure may be copied reprographically for class use.) (Source: Broadbent Drives Limited.)*

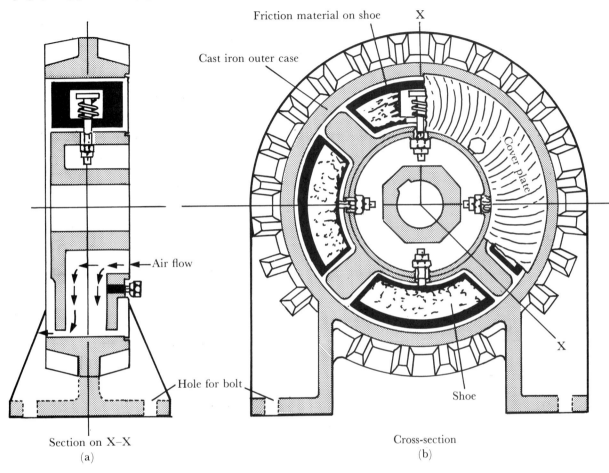

Section on X–X
(a)

Cross-section
(b)

springs is exceeded and the brake shoes move radially outwards. When they touch the outer case, the friction force produces a braking effect.

4.1 Use a photocopy or other type of copy of Figure 4.2 for this exercise.

(a) Identify the main parts of the brake.

(b) On your copy of the diagram, shade in the position in which the shaft would be.

(c) How is the inner part of the brake prevented from slipping around the shaft?

(d) On your copy, using the left-hand diagram, section on X–X, label: the shaft, the metal shoe, the friction material, the retaining spring, and the outer cast iron case.

4.2 When the shaft is rotating at a normal and safe speed, the shoes do not move radially outwards. What provides the centripetal force to keep them in circular motion?

4.3 An emergency arises and the rotation speed goes above the safe value:

(a) Describe what happens to the brake shoe, using the term 'centripetal force'.

(b) When the shoe is touching the cast iron outer case, what are the sources of centripetal force on the shoe?

(c) Does the centripetal force provided by the outer case act radially outwards, radially inwards, or at right-angles to the radius?

4.4 Consider the situation when the brake is operating, and the friction material has been rotating when pressed against the iron outer case. The friction force slows down the rotating machinery:

(a) Describe the main types of energy change which occur.

(b) On your copy of the diagram label the two hottest parts of the brake. These may reach a temperature of about 150 °C.

(c) The outer part of the iron case is a rim with many projections on it. The rim and projections are hot, but not too hot to touch.
(i) What is the purpose of the projections?
(ii) On your copy of the diagram mark in a temperature gradient.

4.5 In Figure 4.2(a) an air flow is marked. What is the purpose of this air flow? (There is no fan for the air. The rotation of the inner unit of the brake causes air to develop an outward movement, and an air flow results.)

4.6 The spring which holds a shoe in position provides a restraining force of 250 N. At slow rotation speeds the spring holds the shoe fixed in its seating.

   Calculate the rotation speed at which the

Figure 4.3 *A metal shoe with its attached brake lining of friction material, in the stationary position inside the outer iron case. The centre of mass, M, of the shoe and brake lining combination, and the axis of rotation, O, are also shown. (The diagram is slightly less than half actual size.)*

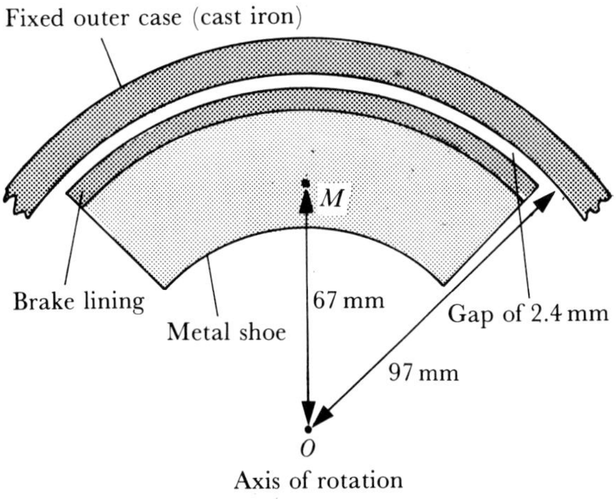

Fixed outer case (cast iron)

Brake lining

Metal shoe

67 mm

Gap of 2.4 mm

97 mm

O

Axis of rotation

shoe starts to move radially outwards. Give the answer in $\mathrm{rad\,s^{-1}}$ and also in $\mathrm{rev\,min^{-1}}$.

Some data   *The mass* of a shoe and its lining combined is 0.314 kg. *The spring constant*: a force of 54.3 N is needed to extend a retaining spring by 1.0 mm. *The brake lining clearance*: when the system is stationary there is a gap of 2.4 mm between the friction material and the iron casing.

4.7 Figure 4.3 shows the distance of the centre of mass of the shoe and lining combination from the axis of rotation. Calculate the rotation speed at which the friction material first touches the iron outer case.

Give the answer in $\mathrm{rad\,s^{-1}}$ and in $\mathrm{rev\,min^{-1}}$.

4.8 Find the radial outwards force which the lining exerts on the iron case at a rotation speed of $1500\,\mathrm{rev\,min^{-1}}$.

4.9 The coefficient of friction between the brake lining material and the iron case is $\mu = 0.5$. Using the answer to Question 4.8, calculate the retarding force which the iron cover exerts on the rotating brake lining of a shoe at $1500\,\mathrm{rev\,min^{-1}}$.

4.10 Using the answer to Question 4.9, find the retarding torque which is produced by the brake lining of one shoe at $1500\,\mathrm{rev\,min^{-1}}$.

4.11 Using the answer to Question 4.10, find the retarding torque produced by the complete brake at $1500\,\mathrm{rev\,min^{-1}}$.

4.12 The brake functions by removing energy from the rotating shaft and its attached machinery. At $1500\,\mathrm{rev\,min^{-1}}$ brake rotation speed, how much energy per second is being removed from the system? (The answer to Question 4.9 or Question 4.10 will help in this calculation.)

4.13 (a) The brake removes energy from the rotating shaft and machinery. In what principal ways is energy then transferred away from the brake?

(b) From what parts of the brake does this principally occur?

(c) At approximately what rate does it occur?

(d) What is the power being removed from the rotating machinery?

Answers to text questions

4.6 $110 \, \text{rad s}^{-1}$, $1000 \, \text{rev min}^{-1}$.

4.7 $130 \, \text{rad s}^{-1}$, $1300 \, \text{rev min}^{-1}$.

4.8 $160 \, \text{N}$.

4.9 $80 \, \text{N}$.

4.10 $7.6 \, \text{Nm}$.

4.11 $30 \, \text{Nm}$.

4.12 $4800 \, \text{J s}^{-1}$.

4.13 (c) $4800 \, \text{J s}^{-1}$; (d) $4.8 \, \text{kW}$.

5. Equilibrium of forces in bridge construction

The bridge

For a system to be stable, all the forces acting on it must balance. Unbalanced forces produce acceleration. Figure 5.1 shows a photograph of a cantilever road bridge, and Figure 5.2 shows an elevation drawing of the bridge. On the left, the road approaches the bridge along an earth embankment. The embankment ends at an abutment, which is a thick wall made of reinforced concrete. The abutment has two functions: one is to act as an end wall to hold back the earth of the embankment;

Figure 5.1 *A cantilever bridge with a suspended centre span. The design engineers had to ensure that all the forces acting on the structure would be balanced. (Designed by the County Engineer's Department, West Sussex County Council; built by Keir Construction Limited.)*

Figure 5.2 *An elevation drawing of the bridge in Figure 5.1. Because the sub-soil was mud and soft clay, the bridge had to be supported on piles standing in the hard chalk rock. Scale, approximately 1:900.*

West   East

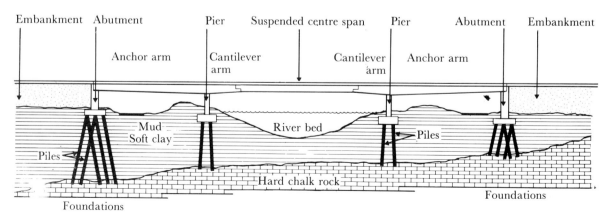

and the other is to hold up the <u>anchor arm</u> of the cantilever system.

In the elevation drawing (Figure 5.2) find the parts that are underlined in the preceding paragraph, and then identify them on the photograph. Also, find and identify the left-hand <u>pier</u>, and the <u>cantilever arm</u>.

The <u>cantilever system</u>, consisting of an anchor arm and a cantilever arm, was constructed as one single reinforced concrete unit, with a mass of about 1400 t. It rests on ball and cup bearings on the pier; these bearings allow the unit to pivot on the pier. The end of the long arm, or anchor arm, rests on bearings on the abutment. The short arm, or cantilever arm, projects beyond the pier and over the river.

On the photograph (Figure 5.1), identify the cantilever unit as a whole.

The sub-soil of mud and soft clay would not support an abutment or a pier; these were thus constructed on <u>piles</u>. Different types of piles can be constructed. These particular piles were of concrete in steel casings. For the west abutment, each pile was made as follows. A steel tube about 18.0 m in length and 0.5 m in diameter had a steel plate welded on to one end, sealing that end of the tube. The steel tube was then hammered down through the clays until the baseplate met the chalk rock. Hammering continued until the base was firmly embedded in the chalk. Concrete was then poured into the upper, open end of the steel tube until this was filled to the level at which the abutment base would be set. Excess steel tube was then cut off with an oxy-acetylene cutter. The result was a leg, or pile, consisting of concrete in a steel case.

In order to support the combined loads of the abutment, the end of the anchor arm and of the expected traffic, and using a safety factor in the design calculations, the design team decided that a total of 27 piles would be needed beneath the abutment. Corresponding structures were designed for, and built on, the east bank of the river.

The centre portion was constructed by lowering beams into place. Each beam had one end resting on the projection of the west cantilever arm, and the other end resting on the projection of the east cantilever arm. Find these parts on the elevation drawing (Figure 5.2). The beams were of reinforced concrete, each having a mass of 27 t and a length of 26 m. A total of 11 beams were needed; and when a reinforced concrete deck had been constructed on them the whole formed a 'suspended centre span' of mass about 500 t. In the photograph (Figure 5.1) identify the suspended centre span.

The stability of an excavator (moments)

Figure 5.3 An excavator designed for digging trenches and holes. To avoid tipping over, anticlockwise moments must be balanced by clockwise moments.

Figure 5.3 shows an excavator which is designed for digging trenches and holes for foundations, and trenches for drains and cables. It has a mass of 12 t and is operated hydraulically. Oil under pressure acts on pistons in the cylinders, and these actuate the arm and the bucket. In Figure 5.3 find the uppermost hydraulic cylinder. It is above the word HYMAC, and it operates the dipper arm. The operating pressure of the oil is 13.3×10^6 Pa, that is, 13.3×10^6 N m^{-2}. Since atmospheric pressure is approximately 0.1×10^6 Pa, the oil pressure is about 133 atmospheres.

5.1 If water were contained in a vertical pipe reaching to a considerable height, what height of water column in the pipe could be supported by a pressure of 13.3×10^6 Pa exerted at the bottom of the pipe? (The pressure at a depth h in a liquid is $p = h\rho g$. The density of water is $\rho = 1000 \text{ kg m}^{-3}$.)

Some idea of the magnitude of the oil pressure is given by the calculation in Question 5.1: the pressure would support a column of water over 1 km high. The oil pressure acts on the face of a piston in the cylinder to produce a force, and this force is used to actuate the dipper arm.

5.2 In the upper cylinder the diameter of the piston is 133 mm, which gives a piston face area of $13.9 \times 10^{-3} \text{ m}^2$:

(a) With an oil pressure of $13.3 \times 10^6 \text{ Pa}$ (Nm^{-2}), what is the force on the piston face?

(b) Because of the high oil pressure, the piston rod is surrounded by packing to prevent oil escaping. The piston rod is highly polished, but in spite of this there is friction between the rod and the surrounding packing. The efficiency of force transfer from the piston face to the outer end of the piston rod is

about 85%. Approximately what force is available for actuating the dipper arm?

It is perhaps difficult to visualise the magnitude of this force. The mass of the excavator is 12 t, or 12 000 kg. Taking the acceleration due to gravity as 10 m s^{-2} gives a weight of $120 \times 10^3 \text{ N}$ for the excavator. The force produced by the piston rod is therefore equivalent to the weight of about $1\frac{1}{3}$ excavators. That is to say, the piston rod, if arranged vertically, could support about $1\frac{1}{3}$ excavators.

Figure 5.4 shows the principal parts of the excavator, with their masses. It also gives the location of each centre of mass and its distance from the slew centreline. What do you think is the meaning of the term 'slew centreline'? For effectiveness in use, the arm and bucket must be able to reach well out. In doing so, however, the excavator must not tip over. For stability, the clockwise moments must be equalled by anticlockwise moments; this consideration must be the basis of the design of the machine.

Figure 5.4 *The principal parts of the excavator in Figure 5.3. For each part, the mass, the position of the centre of mass, and its distance from the slew centreline is given. (This diagram may be photocopied for class use.) (Source: Hymac Limited.)*

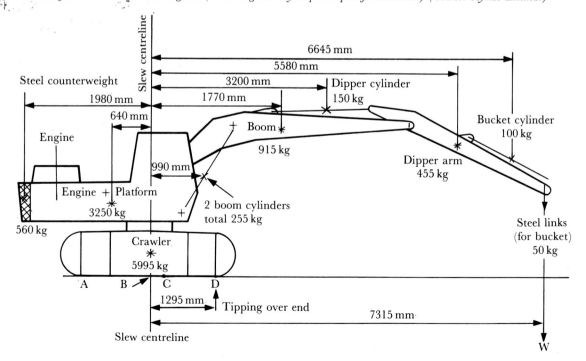

5.3 (a) What do you understand by the 'moment of a force'? Give your answer using a part of the excavator as an example.

(b) Is a moment a scalar or a vector quantity?

(c) Give the dimensions of a moment.

5.4 The engine has been located at the far end of the platform. Why?

5.5 What is the function of the steel counterweight? Why has it been located where it is?

5.6 What is the moment of the dipper arm about the slew centreline, in newton metres? ($g = 10 \, \mathrm{m \, s^{-2}}$)

5.7 What is the moment of the steel counterweight about the slew centreline, in newton metres?

5.8 In Figure 5.4, with the boom and dipper arm stretched out, the moments about the slew centreline are: anticlockwise 31.9×10^3 Nm; clockwise, 59.2×10 N m.

(a) Is the excavator balanced about the slew centreline (and about the point at which the slew centreline meets the ground at B)?

(b) What in practice happens to the excavator so that balance is achieved?

(c) Let C be the point about which the excavator is balanced when its arm is outstretched. On a separate copy of Figure 5.4, mark a vertical dotted line through C. (Do not mark the diagram in the book.)

(i) Through what location, to do with the overall mass of the excavator, must this dotted line pass?

(ii) On the dotted line, mark an approximate position for this location; label it appropriately.

(d) If a bucket is attached to the end of the dipper arm, the excavator tilts further to the right. If it pivots beyond D it tips over completely. Find the mass of bucket and contents which just causes the excavator to tip over completely.

(i) Take moments about D.

(ii) D is a distance of 1295 mm from the slew centreline (see diagram).

(iii) To simplify calculation, engineers sometimes work in 'mass moments' instead of 'force moments'. The mass moment of the steel links (mass 50 kg) about the slew centreline is $50 \, \mathrm{kg} \times 7315 \, \mathrm{mm}$. You may use this method here to find the greatest mass of the bucket and its load which just cause the excavator to tip over completely.

The stability of an abutment (friction; moments)

Look again at Figure 5.2 on page 48 and find the west abutment. Remind yourself of the two main functions of the abutment. These are to hold back the soil of the embankment, and to support the anchor arm of the cantilever system. Figure 5.5 shows a cross-section of the west abutment. It will

Figure 5.5 Cross-section of the west abutment. Scale 1:90. (Source: West Sussex County Council Engineers' Department.)

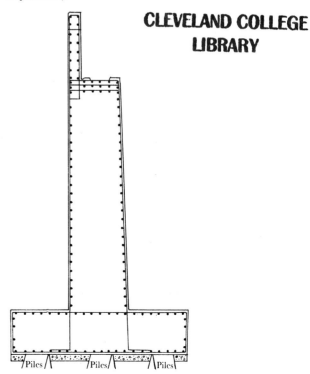

CLEVELAND COLLEGE LIBRARY

Figure 5.6 *The reinforcing steel rods for the main wall of the abutment. (The left-hand structure is temporary scaffolding.)*

Figure 5.7 *A wooden box in the shape of the wall has been formed around the steel rods shown in Figure 5.6. Concrete is being poured into the box.*

be built of reinforced concrete; the dots in the drawing represent the end views of steel reinforcing rods, while the internal lines represent the side views of rods. The piles will project upwards into the base, and the abutment will thus be firmly fixed on to the piles.

5.9 The abutment will be 13 m long. Use the drawing given in Figure 5.5 to obtain an approximate value for the mass of the west abutment, in tonnes. (Regard the main wall as a rectangle. Density of reinforced concrete $= 2.4 \, \text{t m}^{-3}$.)

Figure 5.6 shows steel rods being fixed for the main wall of the abutment. The base has already been made and its upper surface is visible; on the left the scaffolding is standing on the base, and on the right a steelfixer is walking on it.

Fresh concrete is a fluid; a container must therefore be made which has the same dimensions as the wall, and which will contain the fluid concrete until it has set hard. The container is made of wooden boarding and is shown in Figure 5.7. The diagram also shows fresh concrete being

Figure 5.8 *When the concrete has set, the wooden boards are removed. The result is a concrete wall, containing reinforcing rods. Here the anchor arm has also been completed.*

poured into the container from a skip. After two or three days the concrete will have set hard enough for the woodwork to be removed, revealing the concrete structure. Figure 5.8 shows the wall of the west abutment. The cantilever section has also been constructed, and the end of the anchor arm is resting on the abutment.

A simple abutment and its stability

Because the completed abutment is holding back the piled up earth of the embankment, there are pressures on one side of it which are not present on the other side. The abutment might be stable, or it might be pushed along the ground, or it might be tipped over. The forces acting on the abutment, and their possible effects, are shown in Figure 5.9. In Figure 5.9(a), the arrows P_1, P_2, P_3, P_4 and P_5 represent the pressure in the soil of the embankment, the pressure increasing with depth below the surface. These earth pressures acting over the surface of the wall of the abutment produce a thrust, T, acting from left to right.

The weight of the abutment, W, is opposed by an equal and opposite reaction, R, at the base; there is no resultant rce in the vertical direction. A

friction force, F, between the base of the abutment and the ground on which it stands opposes the thrust, T. The abutment might be pushed along the ground by the thrust force, as in Figure 5.9(b); this happens if the thrust force, T, is greater than the limiting friction force, F. The abutment might be tipped over, as in Figure 5.9(c); this happens if the clockwise moments become greater than the anticlockwise moments. The abutment might be stable, which is the case when the thrust force, T, and the friction force, F, are equal and opposite, and the turning moments are equal and opposite.

Will the abutment be pushed along?

Let us calculate whether the simple wall abutment in Figure 5.10 would be pushed along the ground or not. This involves calculating the horizontal forces. These are the thrust, T, and the restraining friction force, F.

The thrust, T, is produced by the earth pressures acting over the inner face of the wall, and is equal to (the average pressure) × (the area of the wall face).

For a freely moving fluid, such as a liquid, of density ρ, the pressure at a depth h is given by

$$p = h\rho g$$

Figure 5.9 *(a) Earth pressure increases with depth below the surface; the forces which act on the abutment are shown. (b) The thrust from the earth pressure pushing the abutment along the ground. (c) The thrust from the earth pressure tipping the abutment over.*

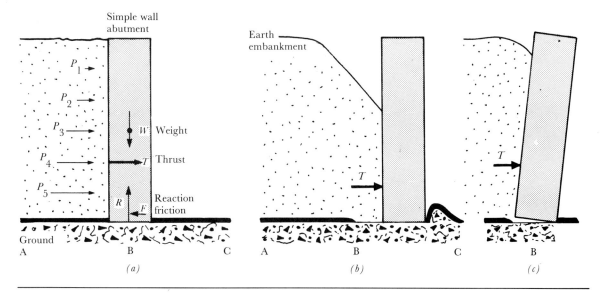

Figure 5.10 *Dimensions for a simple wall abutment.*

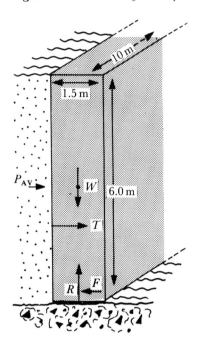

But earth is not a freely moving fluid; it is partially self-supporting, and the pressure which it exerts on a vertical wall is less than that for a liquid of the same density. For soil, a typical factor is about $\frac{1}{3}$. Taking the density of the soil as $2000\,\text{kg m}^{-3}$, the thrust, T, on the wall in Figure 5.10 is given by

$$T = \tfrac{1}{3} \times (\text{average pressure}) \times (\text{area of wall face})$$
$$= \tfrac{1}{3} \times (\tfrac{1}{2} \times 6.0 \times 2000 \times 10) \times (6.0 \times 10)\,\text{N}$$
$$= 1.2 \times 10^{6}\,\text{N}$$

The friction force, F, which resists the thrust is created by the force acting normally between the base of the wall and the ground beneath it; this normal force is the reaction, R, which is equal in magnitude to the weight of the wall, W. Where the coefficient of friction is μ, $F = \mu R$. For soils the coefficient of friction is very variable but a typical example is $\mu = 0.2$. The density of a reinforced concrete wall is about $2400\,\text{kg m}^{-2}$. The weight, W, of the wall is given by

Weight = volume × density of wall ×
  acceleration due to gravity

Now $W = R$ in magnitude, and $F = \mu R$, thus

$$F = \mu R = 0.2 \times (1.5 \times 6.0 \times 10) \times 2400 \times 10\,\text{N}$$
$$= 0.43 \times 10^{6}\,\text{N}$$

So the thrust, $T = 1.6 \times 10^{6}\,\text{N}$, and the resisting friction force, $F = 0.43 \times 10^{6}\,\text{N}$. The resisting force is only about $\frac{1}{4}$ of the thrust, and the wall would be pushed along the ground.

Will the abutment tip over?

Figure 5.11 *The forces which act in a tipping effect on the abutment. (This is the same wall as in Figure 5.10.)*

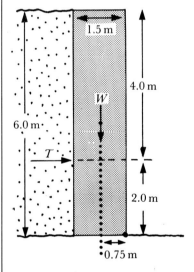

In a fluid of depth h, the average pressure is halfway down, at a depth of $\frac{1}{2}h$. The total thrust can be represented by one resultant, which acts not halfway down but two-thirds of the way down. This is shown for the wall abutment in Figure 5.11. The wall is 6.0 m high, and the thrust resultant acts at a depth of 4.0 m. Its line of action is horizontal. The wall is 1.5 m thick, and the centre of mass is therefore 0.75 m from each side. The line of action of the weight is vertically downwards through the centre of mass, at a distance of 0.75 m from a side. The thrust produces a tendency for the wall to tip or pivot about its right-hand bottom corner. The tipping moment is given by

moment = force × (vertical distance of the line
    of action of the force from the
    pivot)

The line of action of the thrust is at a vertical distance of 2.0 m from the pivot. The line of action of the weight is at a vertical distance of 0.75 m from the pivot. The thrust produces a clockwise tipping moment; the weight produces an anticlockwise moment, which acts to prevent tipping. If the thrust moment (clockwise) exceeds the weight moment (anticlockwise) the wall will tip.

From an earlier calculation:

The thrust T is 1.6×10^6 N
Clockwise moment $= 1.6 \times 10^6$ N $\times 2.0$ m
$= 3.2 \times 10^6$ Nm
Anticlockwise moment $= 2.2 \times 10^6$ N $\times 0.75$ m
$= 1.6 \times 10^6$ Nm

The tipping moment is 3.2×10^6 Nm and the restoring moment is 1.6×10^6 Nm; the wall would therefore tip over.

Designing for stability against tipping

The wall which has been studied so far is easily tipped over by the earth pressure of an embankment. This raises the question of what design would be best, in terms of functional effectiveness and of economy of construction. Figure 5.12 shows four designs. Of the first two designs:

(a) has the dimensions of the main wall of the west abutment of the bridge;
(b) is a simple wall which is twice as thick as design (a).

Designs (c) and (d) are modifications of design (a).

Let us examine the properties of these four designs, with regard to resisting tipping.

5.10 The west abutment of the bridge shown in Figures 5.1 and 5.2 is 13 m long. In our calculations for the wall in Figure 5.12 we will use a length of 13 m so that the results will relate directly to the bridge abutment. The main wall of the bridge abutment is 6.6 m high and 1.4 m thick; we will use these values in the designs.

Some data

Mass of the basic wall (a) $= 300$ t
Weight of the basic wall $= 3.0 \times 10^6$ N
Density of reinforced concrete $= 2400$ kg m^{-3}
Density of soil of embankment $= 2000$ kg m^{-3}
Horizontal pressure correction factor for soil $= \frac{1}{3}$

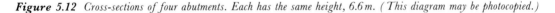

Figure 5.12 Cross-sections of four abutments. Each has the same height, 6.6 m. (This diagram may be photocopied.)

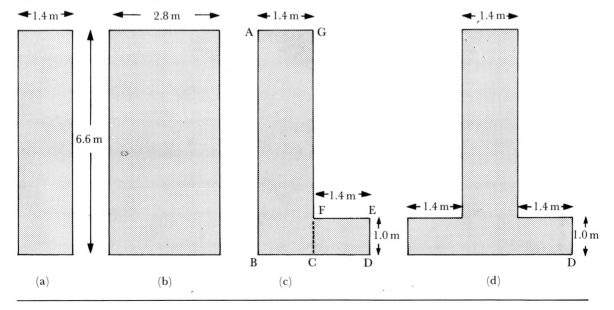

Either use a copy of Figure 5.12 or sketch the designs on a sheet of paper. Take the embankment as being on the left of the wall.

(a) *Abutment design (a)*

  (i) Mark in the position and line of action of the earth thrust resultant on the wall.

  (ii) Calculate the magnitude of the thrust.

  (iii) Calculate the overturning moment.

  (iv) Calculate the restoring moment due to the weight of the wall.

(b) *Abutment design (b)*

  (i) Is the earth thrust on the wall the same as for design (a), or is it different?

  (ii) State the overturning moment.

  (iii) Calculate the restoring moment.

  (iv) Will the wall be tipped over?

  (v) What factor of safety is there?

  (vi) What mass of reinforced concrete was needed in design (a); what mass in design (b)?

  (vii) Comment on (vi) in terms of the cost, and in terms of the space occupied by the structure.

(c) *Abutment design (c)*

  (i) State the overturning moment about the corner D as pivot.

  (ii) Calculate the restoring moment due to the column ABCG.

  (iii) Compare this restoring moment with the one in design (a), which is an identical column. Why is the moment greater in design (c)?

  (iv) Calculate the restoring moment due to the projecting part CDEF.

  (v) Calculate the total restoring moment.

  (vi) Would the abutment be overturned?

  (vii) What factor of safety is there?

  (viii) Has the design any advantages over design (b)?

(d) *Abutment design (d)*

In design (c) the foot of the basic wall was provided with a toe, to the right. In design (d) the foot of the wall is again provided with a toe, and also with a heel to the left. Any tilting would take place about the toe

at D. On your own copy of Figure 5.12(d) shade in the soil of the embankment. Because there is soil to the left of the heel, the line faction of the soil thrust is still at a point 2.2 m above the base of the wall; and it has the same magnitude as before. There is a column of soil above the heel.

Some data

Weight of soil column above the heel $= 2.0 \times 10^6$ N

Weight of concrete heel $= 0.44 \times 10^6$ N

  (i) Calculate the restoring moment of the heel, about D.

  (ii) Calculate the restoring moment of the column of soil, about D.

  (iii) Calculate the total restoring moment for the whole structure, about D. (For this, use your earlier answer about design(c).)

  (iv) Would the structure be stable against tipping?

  (v) What safety factor is there?

(e) (i) Suggest which is the best design out of designs (a)–(d). Justify your choice by taking into account economy in materials and safety factors.

  (ii) Which design did the design engineers use for the bridge abutment? (Examine Figure 5.5.)

A bridge cantilever (moments; reactions at supports)

Figure 5.13 shows the west cantilever section of the bridge illustrated in Figure 5.1. Look again at Figure 5.1 and find the west cantilever. Also, look at Figure 5.2 and find the west abutment and the west pier. In the completed bridge the cantilever unit has a mass of about 1500 t, and it supports one end of the centre span, which has a mass of 500 t. The weights of these units exert large downward forces on the pier and the abutment. In order to design an appropriately strong pier and found-

Figure 5.13 *The west cantilever section of the bridge in Figure 5.1. Between the pier and the cantilever are five ball and cup bearings on which the cantilever pivots.*

ations, and an appropriately strong abutment and foundations, it is necessary to know the magnitude of the downward forces on them. These forces can be found by using the principle of moments.

The cantilever unit is supported by two upward forces. There is an upward force on its left-hand end where this rests on the abutment; this force is labelled *F*. There is an upward force on it at the bearings, where these rest on the pier; this force is labelled *G*. For the cantilever unit to be in equilibrium, the sum of the vertically upward forces must equal the sum of the vertically downward forces:

$$F + G = 11\,\text{MN} + 3\,\text{MN}$$
$$F + G = 14\,\text{MN}$$

For the cantilever unit to be in equilibrium, the sum of the clockwise moments about the pivot at P must equal the sum of the anticlockwise moments.

Clockwise moments	*Anticlockwise moments*
$(F \times 25\,\text{m}) + (3\,\text{MN} \times 3\,\text{m})$	$= 11\,\text{MN} \times 11\,\text{m}$
$F \times 25\,\text{m} + 9\,\text{MN m}$	$= 121\,\text{MN m}$
$F \times 25\,\text{m}$	$= 112\,\text{MN m}$

from which $F = 4.48\,\text{MN}$ upwards.

Thus the supporting force, *F*, provided by the abutment is 4.5 MN upwards. Now the sum of this upward force, *F*, and the upward force *G* at the pier is

$$F + G = 14\,\text{MN}$$
$$\therefore 4.48\,\text{MN} + G = 14\,\text{MN};$$
$$G = 9.52\,\text{MN}\ \text{upward.}$$

Figure 5.14 *The west cantilever unit supported on its abutment and pier. The unit itself, without road surface, has a mass of 1400 t: 1100 t in the anchor arm, and 300 t in the cantilever arm.*

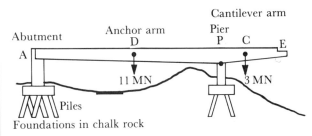

Figure 5.15 *The vertical forces acting on the cantilever unit.*

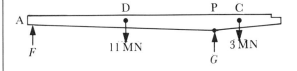

Figure 5.16 *The vertical forces acting about the bearings as pivot, at P.*

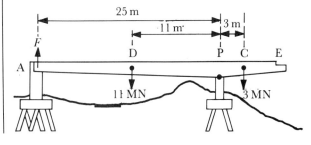

Figure 5.17 *The centre span in position. Also shown are the vertical forces acting on the cantilever about the pivot at P.*

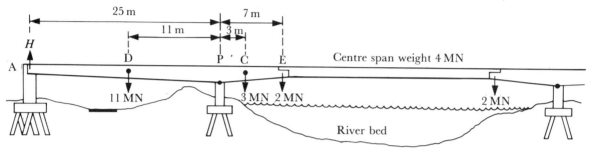

Thus the supporting force, *G*, provided by the pier is 9.5 MN upward.

After the east and west cantilever units were built, the centre span was then constructed. This was done by lowering 11 reinforced concrete beams into the gap over the river, between the ends of the cantilever arms, so that one end of each beam rested on the west cantilever arm and the other end on the east arm. A deck of reinforced concrete was then constructed on the 11 beams. The mass of this centre span with its concrete deck (but without a bituminous road surface) was 400 t, giving a weight of 4 MN. This produced a downward force of 2 MN on the end of each cantilever arm.

5.11 For this stage, when the centre span was in place, find the downward force on the abutment and on the pier. To do this, find the upward reaction, *H*, at the abutment and at the pier. Proceed as follows:
(a) Draw a free body diagram for the cantilever unit, and mark in the vertical forces which act on it.
(b) Produce an equation for the sum of the upward forces.
(c) Take moments about the pivot, P, and find the magnitude of force, *H*, at the abutment end.
(d) Using your equation from (b), find the upward force on the bearings at the pivot, P.
(e) State:
   (i) the force on the abutment due to the superstructure;
   (ii) the force on the pier due to the superstructure.

5.12 To provide a road surface on the concrete decks of the cantilever units and of the centre span, stone chippings coated with bituminous material were laid and rolled. These layers increased the masses of the units, to give final weights of: anchor arm, 12 MN; cantilever arm, 3.3 MN; centre span, 5 MN. For the completed bridge, find:
(a) the force acting down on the abutment;
(b) the force acting down on the pier.

A jib crane (components of a force; resultant of forces)

The engineers responsible for lifting the beams and placing them had to ensure that the lifting cables would safely support the load of 27 t. They thus needed to find the tension in each cable. The designers of the crane had to ensure that the steel lattice jib would safely carry the maximum load which the crane was intended to lift. This involved finding the thrust in the jib, for the maximum load, at various angles of the jib to the vertical.

5.13 Study Figure 5.18. State whether the following are in *tension* or in *compression*:
(a) the suspended beam;
(b) a lifting cable attached to the beam;
(c) the vertical cables which go through the pulley block;
(d) the steel lattice jib;
(e) the two tie wires to the right of the jib;
(f) the steel strut attached to the foot of the jib;
(g) the two steel ties attached to the rear of the crane.

Figure 5.18 *The mobile jib crane is positioning a beam for the centre span of the bridge. Each beam is 26 m long and has a mass of 27 t. (This photograph may be photocopied.)*

5.14 Find the tension in a lifting cable attached to the beam. The beam has a mass of 27 000 kg:

(a) Sketch a free body diagram of the beam, and mark in the forces which act on it.

(b) Consider either the right-hand or the left-hand suspension point for the beam. What is the magnitude of the vertically downward force at this point?

(c) The tension in the cable must have a *vertically upward component* which is equal in magnitude to the downward force at the beam attachment. The tension in the cable must also have a *horizontal component*, which compresses the beam. Draw a sketch of the end of the beam, and mark in *the point of action* and the *direction* of *the tension in the cable*, its *vertical component*, and its *horizontal component*.

(d) (i) Sketch a triangle of forces, and mark in the magnitude of the vertically downward force: 135 kN.

(ii) On a copy of Figure 5.18, measure the

angle that the cable makes with the vertical (or the horizontal). (Do not mark the photograph in the book.)
(iii) Mark the angle on the sketch.
(e) Find:
(i) the tension in the cable;
(ii) the magnitude of the horizontal component (which is acting to compress the beam).

These can be done either by calculation or by a scale drawing. For a drawing, a scale of 10 mm:10 kN would be convenient; the drawing could be done directly on to a copy of Figure 5.18.

5.15 For the crane in Figure 5.18, find the thrust in the jib, and the total tension in the tie wires which run back from the top of the jib. Proceed as follows, using a copy of Figure 5.18:

(a) For the vertical cables, draw a line through the hook, the pulley block, and the centre of the pulley projection at the top of the jib, and continue the line upwards

(b) For the jib, draw a line through the pivot at the base and through the top of the lattice-work, and continue the line upwards.

(c) For the tie wires, draw a line as closely as possible between the two of them, and continue the line upwards. The three lines meet at a point just beyond the top of the jib (because of uncertainties as to precisely where to draw the lines, these may not meet at a point but may intersect to form a small triangle).

(d) The weight of the beam is 270 kN. Draw a triangle of forces to scale. A scale of 20 mm:100 kN will be convenient.

(e) Find (i) the thrust in the jib, and (ii) the total tension in the two tie wires.

Answers to text questions

5.1 1330 m, or 1.3 km.

5.2 (a) 185×10^3 N; (b) 157×10^3 N.

5.6 $[M][L]^2[T]^{-2}$

5.6 25.4×10^3 Nm, clockwise.

5.7 11.1 Nm, anticlockwise.

5.8 (a) No; (b) The excavator tips forward towards the right. Some track at end A lifts off the ground, and on the right some track moves down into contact with the ground; (c)(i) the centre of mass; (d) 2070 kg, or 2.07 t.

5.9 400 t.

5.10 (a)(ii) 1.9×10^6 N; (iii) 4.2×10^6 Nm clockwise. (iv) 2.1×10^6 Nm anticlockwise. (b)(i) the same; (ii) 4.2×10^6 Nm clockwise; (iii) 8.4×10^6 Nm anticlockwise; (iv) No; (v) 2. (c)(i) 4.2×10^6 Nm clockwise; (ii) 6.3×10^6 Nm anticlockwise; (iv) 0.31×10^6 Nm anticlockwise; (v) 6.6×10^6 Nm anticlockwise; (vi) No; (vii) 1.5. (d)(i) 1.5×10^6 Nm anticlockwise; (ii) 7.0×10^6 Nm anticlockwise; (iii) 15×10^6 Nm anticlockwise; (iv) yes; (v) 3.6.

5.11 (c) $H = 3.9$ MN upwards; (d) 12.1 MN upwards; (e)(i) 3.9 MN downwards; (ii) 12.1 MN downwards.

5.12 (a) 4.2 MN downwards; (b) 13.6 MN downwards.

5.13 (a) compression; (b) tension; (c) tension; (d) compression; (e) tension; (f) compression; (g) tension.

5.14 (b) 135 000 N (135 kN); (e)(i) 160 kN (range 157 kN–163 kN).

5.15 (e)(i) 900 kN (range 880 kN–920 kN); (ii) 700 kN (range 680 kN–720 kN).

6. Pile driving

Energy and momentum in pile driving

Figures 6.1 and 6.2 show the early work carried out on the west abutment of the bridge which is illustrated in Figures 5.1 and 5.2, page 48.

The suspended mass in Figure 6.1 is a drop hammer. By virtue of its height above ground level it possesses gravitational potential energy. If the hammer is dropped, it gains speed; potential energy is changed into kinetic energy. The kinetic energy can be used to drive down a pile.

The tubular steel pile case in Figure 6.2 is about 20 m long, and the photograph shows the bottom 4 m together with bottom supports. The lower end of the tube has a steel plate welded on to it, closing the end of the tube and forming a base. (This is out of sight, just below ground level.)

A crane operator manoeuvres the 4 t hammer into the open top of the pile case, lowers it slowly down the tube, and then allows it to drop the final distance, which is usually about 1 m. When the

Figure 6.2 A tubular pile case, ready to be driven down.

Figure 6.1 Gravitational potential energy. A 4 t drop hammer.

hammer hits the base plate its momentum is shared with that of the pile case; and the hammer and pile case move down together, with the momentum being conserved.

The downward movement of the pile case is opposed by the friction of the soil against the outer surface of the case; downward movement continues until the work done against the friction force equals the amount of kinetic energy possessed by the case and hammer combination at the start of their joint motion.

In this section we consider the questions: How much potential energy is possessed by a drop hammer? When a drop hammer hits a base plate, with what velocity does it hit the plate? When a pile case and hammer combination begin to move down, what is their joint initial velocity? Is energy conserved in the motions? How far down might a pile be driven by one hammer blow?

Energy and speed of a drop hammer

Gravitational potential energy

In Figure 6.1 the hammer has gravitational potential energy. In lifting the hammer from ground level to a height, h, above ground level, work is done on the hammer against the force of its weight.

$$\begin{aligned} \text{Work done} &= \text{force} \times \text{distance moved in the} \\ &\quad \text{direction of the force} \\ &= \text{weight} \times \text{height above ground} \\ &\quad \text{level} \\ &= mg \times h \\ &= mgh \end{aligned}$$

The work done on the mass remains in the system as gravitational potential energy.

If the 4 t hammer shown in Figure 6.1 is raised a distance of 10 m above ground level, it acquires gravitational potential energy which is given by

$$\begin{aligned} \text{Potential energy} = mgh &= 4000 \times 10 \times 10 \text{ J} \\ &= 400 \times 10^3 \text{ J} \end{aligned}$$

and the potential energy possessed is 400 kJ.

Kinetic energy, and speed

If the mass is dropped freely it accelerates downwards, and at the moment of hitting the ground (the original reference level) the potential energy has returned to zero and the energy has been transformed into kinetic energy. If the speed of the hammer is v, its kinetic energy is $KE = \frac{1}{2}mv^2$ and

$$\begin{aligned} \tfrac{1}{2}mv^2 &= mgh \\ v^2 &= 2gh \\ v &= \sqrt{(2gh)} \end{aligned}$$

The speed of the hammer on hitting the ground is therefore independent of its mass; it is a function of the acceleration due to gravity, and of its original height above ground level.

Considering the 4 t hammer raised to a height of 10 m above ground level, its free-fall speed on striking the ground would be

$$\begin{aligned} v &= \sqrt{(2 \times 10 \times 10)} = \sqrt{(200)} \\ &= 14 \text{ m s}^{-1} \end{aligned}$$

6.1 In driving tubular piles with a drop hammer, the vertical drop distance for the hammer is restricted to about 1 m (to avoid knocking the base plate off the tube). Taking the base plate of the pile as the reference level, and a drop height of 0.8 m, calculate the speed of the hammer on impact.

The hammer and pile case combination after impact

The 4 t hammer hits the base of the pile case with a speed of 4 m s^{-1} (after a drop of 0.8 m). The pile case has a mass of 2 t. In the collision, momentum is conserved. Therefore:

Momentum of hammer immediately before collision	=	momentum of (hammer + pile case) immediately after collision

If the mass and velocity of the hammer are M and V, respectively, if the mass of the pile case is m, and if the velocity of the combination immediately after impact is v, then

Total momentum = total momentum
before impact   after impact

$(MV) + (m \times 0) = (M + m)v$

$(4 \times 4) + (2 \times 0) = (4 + 2)v$

$\frac{16}{6} = v$ and $v = 2.7 \, \text{m s}^{-1}$

and the velocity of the combination immediately after impact is $3 \, \text{m s}^{-1}$ downwards.

6.2 Is momentum a scalar or a vector quantity?

6.3 Give the dimensions of momentum.

6.4 A 1 t pile is held lightly in position and hit by a 2 t hammer travelling with a velocity of $5 \, \text{m s}^{-1}$ downwards. With what velocity does the pile and hammer combination start moving?

6.5 A 2 t pile is hit by a 3 t hammer travelling with a velocity of $6 \, \text{m s}^{-1}$ downwards. With what velocity does the pile and hammer combination start moving?

Kinetic energy before and after impact

In the impact and subsequent movement of hammer and pile case, momentum is conserved. Is kinetic energy conserved?

6.6 Use the example of the hammer and pile case given in the preceding section (speed of a hammer and pile case combination after impact, page 62) to find whether kinetic energy is conserved:

(a) What was the kinetic energy of the hammer immediately before impact?

(b) What was the kinetic energy of the hammer and pile case combination immediately after impact?

(c) Was kinetic energy conserved?

(d) Approximately what fraction of the original kinetic energy was lost?

(e) Suggest ways in which the lost kinetic energy was used up.

Stopping distance of a hammered pile

In order to construct the west pier of the bridge illustrated in Figure 5.2, page 48, digging had to be

Figure 6.3 *A length of sheet piling being driven down. The hammer is operated by compressed air. A box-shaped cofferdam is being constructed, within which to dig below the river water level.*

done below the water level of the river. To prevent river water seeping into the trench and to prevent the sides of the trench from falling in, a watertight steel box was constructed around the site for the trench. Lengths of steel sheet were hammered down, each sheet interlocking with the next by means of a tongue and groove arrangement. Each sheet was hammered down until its foot was embedded in the chalk bedrock. Such a box-like structure, formed to enable work to take place within it, is known as a cofferdam.

The photograph in Figure 6.3 shows the cofferdam being made for the west pier. Each steel sheet is 15 m long and has a mass of 0.8 t.

The hammer consists of two main parts. There is a massive steel body, with a mass of about 2.5 t, which is clamped to the top of the sheet that is being hammered. Inside the body is a piston or ram with a mass of about $\frac{1}{3}$ t. The ram is raised inside the body by means of compressed air. At the top of its upward travel, a set of valves operates and compressed air accelerates the ram downwards until it strikes the outer body with the attached steel sheet, hammering them both down. The process is then repeated.

Although the mass of the ram is less than that of typical *drop* hammers ($\frac{1}{3}$ t contrasted with 3 t or 4 t) its velocity on impact is comparable, because of the effect of the compressed air. Moreover, the hammering rate is very much higher: in the region of

Figure 6.4 *A length of steel sheet pile being hammered into the ground. After a hammer blow, the moving pile and attached hammer are brought to rest by friction between the pile and the soil.*

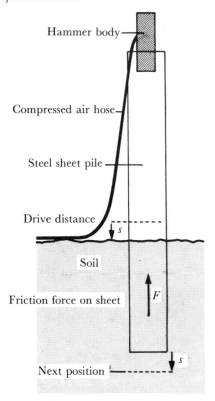

200 blows per minute, contrasted with around 2 blows per minute for a crane-operated drop hammer.

In Figure 6.4 a length of steel pile has been hammered some way into the ground. If the mass of the entire hammer is M and the mass of the steel pile is m, and if after a blow by the interior ram the whole system moves down with an initial speed of v, the kinetic energy of the system is

$$KE = \tfrac{1}{2}(M+m)v^2$$

The pile moves against the friction force which is caused by the soil in contact with the steel sheet. If the sheet moves down a distance s, and if the average friction force during that movement is F, then the work done by the pile moving against the friction force is

Work done $= F \times s$

When all the kinetic energy has been used in performing this work, the pile and hammer come to rest. At that stage:

$$\frac{\text{Initial kinetic energy}}{\text{of combination}} = \frac{\text{total work done}}{\text{against soil friction}}$$

$$\tfrac{1}{2}(M+m)v^2 = Fs$$

The friction force which resists the movement of the pile depends upon the *surface area of the steel sheet* which is below ground, and upon *the nature of the soil*. At this site the friction force was about $10\,000\,\mathrm{N\,m^{-2}}$ of buried surface area of steel sheet.

Let us take an example from the west pier piling.

Data

Surface area of sheet pile per metre *length* of pile $= 1.2\,\mathrm{m^2}$ (this includes both sides of the sheet)

Friction force per unit area of sheet at soil/sheet boundary $= 10\,000\,\mathrm{N\,m^{-2}}$

Kinetic energy of the steel sheet and the attached hammer as both move down together after a blow $= 480\,\mathrm{J}$ (480 Nm)

Buried length of pile, so far $= 2.0\,\mathrm{m}$

At the next blow, how far down will the sheet move?

$$\frac{\text{Kinetic energy}}{\text{of combination}} = \frac{\text{Friction force} \times}{\text{distance moved}}$$

$$480\,\mathrm{Nm} = (2.0\,\mathrm{m} \times 1.2\,\mathrm{m^2\,m^{-1}} \times 10\,000\,\mathrm{Nm^{-2}}) \times s$$

$$\frac{480\,\mathrm{m}}{2.4 \times 10^4} = s = 20 \times 10^{-3}\,\mathrm{m}$$

Thus the pile moves down a distance of 20 mm.

This may seem a small distance, but as the ram is delivering about 200 blows per minute it represents a downward drive rate of about (200×20) $\mathrm{mm\,min^{-1}}$ or $4\,\mathrm{m\,min^{-1}}$, at the time of that particular blow.

After each blow, however, there is a greater area of sheet below ground level, and the friction force increases in proportion. Thus each successive blow achieves a smaller drive distance, and the drive rate decreases.

6.7 Find the drive distance for a sheet pile at the west pier area when it receives one blow from the ram of a British Steel Piling Company's number 700 N hammer, when 5 m of the pile are below ground level:

Pile data
Length = 15.0 m
Mass = 53.3 kg per metre length
Surface area = 1.2 m^2 per metre length

Friction data
Friction force = 10.0 kN m^{-2} of buried pile surface area

Hammer data, no. 700 N hammer
Mass of hammer body = 2620 kg
Mass of internal ram = 380 kg
Velocity of ram on striking hammer body = 5.8 m s^{-1} downwards

Proceed as follows:
(a) Find the mass of the pile.
(b) Using the conservation of momentum principle, find the velocity with which the combination of pile, hammer body and ram set off immediately after the ram hits the body.
(c) Find the kinetic energy of the combination at the moment at which it starts to move downwards.
(d) Equate the kinetic energy with the work which is done in moving the pile through the unknown drive distance *s* against the force of soil friction. Find the drive distance *s*.

6.8 A steel sheet pile identical to that in Question 6.7 has a length of 6 m buried, and it is being driven down by a British Steel Piling Company No. 900 N hammer. For one blow from the ram, how far down does the pile go?

Hammer data, No. 900 N hammer
Mass of hammer body = 4330 kg
Mass of ram = 730 kg
Velocity of ram on striking the hammer body = 5.8 m s^{-1} downwards

Pile data and friction data
As in Question 6.7.

Proceed in stages as in Question 6.7

Answers to text questions

6.1 4 m s^{-1}.
6.2 vector.
6.3 [M][L][T]$^{-1}$.
6.4 3.3 m s^{-1} downwards.
6.5 3.6 m s^{-1} downwards.
6.6 (a) 30 kJ (32 kJ); (b) 20 kJ (22 kJ); (c) No; (d) $\frac{1}{3}$.
6.7 (a) 800 kg; (b) 0.58 m s^{-1}; (c) 640 J; (d) 11 mm.
6.8 (a) 800 kg; (b) 0.83 m s^{-1} downwards; (c) 1.7 kJ or 1.8 kJ; (d) 24 mm.

7. Power transmission by belt drives

Belt drives

Figure 7.1 *In the foreground is shown an electric motor driving a vacuum pump in a paper-making mill. The motor is transmitting 30 kW of power to the pump by means of a flat belt. (Source: Stephens Miraclo Extremultus Limited.)*

Of all the power used by industry, over 50% of it goes to supply electric motors which drive machinery. Power has to be transferred from the motor to the machinery, and this is often done by means of a belt drive. Figure 7.1 shows an electric motor transferring 30 kW of power to a vacuum pump by means of a belt drive.

Well-designed and well-manufactured flat belt drives can transfer power from a motor to a machine with 98% efficiency. V-shaped belt drives are much less efficient; those used in vehicles for driving the dynamo, water pump and radiator fan are about 80% efficient. When a V-belt reaches a pulley it has to be forced into the pulley groove; and then on leaving, it has to be pulled out of the groove. Energy is used in each process.

The structure of a flat belt drive

Figure 7.2 *The structure of a high-efficiency flat belt. (Source: Stephens Miraclo Extremultus Limited.)*

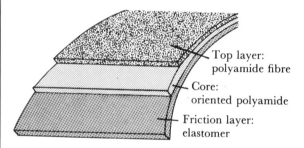

Top layer: polyamide fibre

Core: oriented polyamide

Friction layer: elastomer

Two essential parts to a belt drive are (a) the pulleys, and (b) the belt.

The *pulleys* are usually of cast iron; but if the peripheral speed is high, then steel will be needed. The pulleys have to be machined to a very high standard, and 'crowned' to keep the belt central on the pulley.

The *belt* consists of two essential parts: the *friction member* which transfers the drive from the pulley to the belt; and the *tension member* which carries the load. Figure 7.2 shows these. The lower layer consists of an elastomer providing a high coefficient of friction with steel. The middle layer consists of polyamide, with the molecules highly oriented along the length of the layer: giving it a high resistance to stretching and a high tensile strength.

The belt in Figure 7.2 also has a top layer, which is of polyamide fabric; its function is simply to improve the visual appearance of the belt.

Look again at the sectional diagram of a belt in Figure 7.2, and go over the function of each layer, and the nature of the material that has been chosen to enable it to perform that function.

Power transfer

Figure 7.3 *The tensions in the upper and lower parts of a belt when a belt drive is stationary (a), and when it is moving and driving a machine (b).*

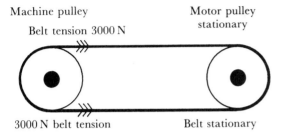

(a) System stationary

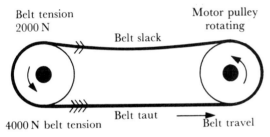

(b) System moving

When the drive is stationary the tension in the upper length of the belt is the same as that in the lower length of the belt. This is shown in Figure 7.3(a), where tension in the upper length is shown as 3000 N and in the lower length as 3000 N also.

When the motor pulley rotates, one part of the belt becomes more taut and the other becomes less taut. That is, the tension increases in one part of the belt and decreases in the other part. This is shown in Figure 7.3(b) where the motor pulley is rotating anticlockwise and the tension in the lower part of the belt has *increased* from 3000 N to 4000 N, and in the upper part of the belt it has *decreased* from 3000 N to 2000 N.

Between the lower belt and the upper belt there is a difference in tension of (4000 N − 2000 N), that is, 2000 N. As the lower part of the belt moves, a resultant force of 2000 N moves in the direction of belt travel. When the belt moves along a distance of 1 m, the work done is

Work done = force × distance moved in the direction of the force
= 2000 N × 1 m
= 2000 Nm = 2000 J

and the belt does 2000 J of work on the machine.

Figure 7.4 *The belt speed and tensions in a belt driving a machine.*

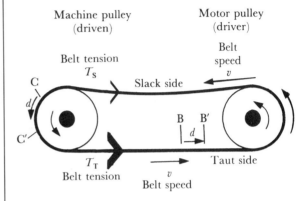

In Figure 7.4 the motor pulley is rotating anticlockwise, and thus the lower part of the belt is more taut than the upper part. The resultant force doing work on the machine is

$$\text{Force} = (T_\text{T} - T_\text{S}).$$

If, on the machine pulley, a point C on the belt moves round to a point C′ through a distance d, and at the same time on the lower part of the belt a point S moves to S′ through a distance d, then the work done on the machine is

Work done = force × distance moved in the direction of the force
$$W = (T_\text{T} - T_\text{S}) \times d$$

If the belt moves this distance d in a time t then the rate of working is

$$\frac{\text{Work done}}{\text{Time taken}} = \frac{(T_\text{T} - T_\text{S}) \times d}{t}$$

But d/t is the distance moved by the belt divided by the time taken, and it is the belt speed, v. And

$$\frac{\text{Work done}}{\text{Time taken}} = (T_\text{T} - T_\text{S}) \times v$$

Now, the work done divided by the time taken is the power transferred. Thus the power transferred depends on the *difference in the belt tensions* and on the *belt speed*, and it is the product of these quantities.

Figure 7.1 shows in the foreground a belt drive which is transferring power to a vacuum pump. The manufacturer of the belt gives the following operating data:

Tension of belt, tight side, $T_T = 2950\,\text{N}$
Tension of belt, slack side, $T_S = 1250\,\text{N}$
Belt speed $= 17.7\,\text{m s}^{-1}$

From this we can calculate the power which is being transferred:

$$P = (T_T - T_S) \times v$$
$$= (2950\,\text{N} - 1250\,\text{N}) \times 17.7\,\text{m s}^{-1}$$
$$= 1700\,\text{N} \times 17.7\,\text{m s}^{-1}$$
$$= 30\,090\,\text{J s}^{-1}$$
$$= 30\,100\,\text{W}$$

Thus the belt is transferring 30 kW of power.

7.1 The photograph in Figure 7.1 shows vacuum pumps being driven by electric motors using belt drives. Find the power which is being transmitted to the second vacuum pump. The manufacturer of the belt gives the following operating information for pump no. 2:

Tension of belt, tight side $= 7880\,\text{N}$
Tension of belt, slack side $= 3320\,\text{N}$
Belt speed $= 20.4\,\text{m s}^{-1}$

7.2 In the motor and pump system described in Question 7.1, when the motor was off and the belt was stationary the belt tension was 5600 N. That is, the tension in the upper part of the belt was 5600 N and in the lower part of the belt it was 5600 N:
(a) What was the change in tension of the belt on the tight side when the operating conditions had been reached?
(b) What was the change in tension in the slack part of the belt?
(c) Comment on your finding.

7.3 In the photograph in Figure 7.1, operating data for the front pump was given in the text

example on page 68. Additional information is that the tension in the stationary belt is 2100 N. Comment on these figures for tensions.

Centripetal force and belt drives

Figure 7.5 *(a) A small part of a belt passing round a pulley. (b) The tension, T_o, downwards in the belt resolved into a radial component, C.*

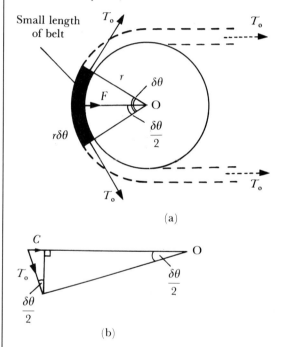

Consider a small length of belt which is passing round a pulley. The direction of motion of the chosen small length is being changed as it passes round the circumference of the pulley. In order to keep the length in circular motion, a force must be applied to it in a direction which is radially inwards. This force is represented in Figure 7.5(a) as force F, the centripetal force.

The only source from which this force can come is the tension, T_o, in the belt. Let us find this force.

In Figure 7.5(a) the small length of belt subtends an angle $\delta\theta$ at the centre, O, of the pulley. The lower half of the bit subtends an angle $\frac{1}{2}\delta\theta$ at the centre, O.

(1) Let us find the centripetal force, F, needed to keep the belt in circular motion on the pulley. Let the mass per unit length of belt be m and the belt speed by v.

In Figure 7.5(a), the length of the bit of belt is $r\delta\theta$. Its mass is therefore $mr\delta\theta$. The centripetal force, F, required to hold it in circular motion is therefore

$$F = \frac{(mr\delta\theta)v^2}{r} = m\delta\theta v^2$$

(2) Let us find the contribution which the lower tension, T_o, makes to the centripetal force.

In Figure 7.5(b) the tension T_o has been resolved into a radially inwards component, C. If the bit of belt is very small, then $\delta\theta$ is very small, and $\delta\theta/2$ is very small; and therefore $\sin\delta\theta/2 = \delta\theta/2$:

$$C = T_o\sin\delta\theta/2$$
$$= T_o\delta\theta/2$$

The upper tension, T_o, provides an equal contribution C radially inwards, and the total is

$$C + C = 2C = 2T_o\delta\theta/2 = T_o\delta\theta$$
$$\therefore\ 2C = T_o\delta\theta$$

(3) We will now equate the required centripetal force, F, found in (1), with the total available, $2C$, from the tension:

$$F = 2C$$
$$m\delta\theta v^2 = T_o\delta\theta$$
$$\therefore\ mv^2 = T_o$$

Thus, simply to cause a moving belt to pass round a pulley, without doing any work on a machine, requires additional tension in the belt; this tension force is needed to change the direction of motion of the mass of that part of the belt which is on the pulley as it passes round the pulley. For the belt then to do work on a machine, additional tension is required in the belt.

7.4 In the photograph in Figure 7.1, the belt in the front drive system has a mass per unit length of $0.27\ \mathrm{kg\,m^{-1}}$, and it travels at a speed of $17.7\ \mathrm{m\,s^{-1}}$. Find the tension needed in the belt in order to make it travel round a pulley.

7.5 In the photograph in Figure 7.1, the belt in the second drive system from the front has a mass per unit length of $0.63\ \mathrm{kg\,m^{-1}}$, and it travels at a speed of $20.4\ \mathrm{m\,s^{-1}}$. Find the tension needed in the belt in order to make it travel round the pulleys.

Friction and belt drives

Figure 7.6 *The angles of contact of a belt on two pulleys, θ_1 on the larger pulley and θ_2 on the smaller.*

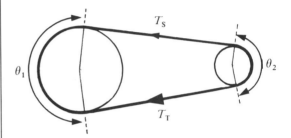

For a belt drive to turn a machine pulley, force must be transferred from the belt to the pulley. This is achieved by the friction force between the belt and the pulley surface.

The belt is kept in contact with the pulley surface by the tension in the belt. If a part of the belt is pressing on to the pulley surface with a force R normal to the surface (that is, a force R inwards radially) then the force F which is being transferred tangentially to the pulley surface is

$F = \mu R$ where μ is the coefficient of friction

To be effective, the belt must not slip. The tension on the taut side, T_T, must not be so much greater than the tension on the slack side, T_S, that slipping occurs. And for force transfer to occur, the belt must be in contact with a sufficient part of the circumference. The latter is conveniently measured as the angle of contact, θ, which is the angle subtended at the centre of the pulley by the length of belt in contact with the circumference. This is shown in Figure 7.6.

As T_T increases and T_S decreases, the ratio T_T/T_S increases:

When $\dfrac{T_T}{T_S} = e^{\mu\theta}$ the belt is about to slip

When $\dfrac{T_T}{T_S} > e^{\mu\theta}$ the belt slips

7.6 (a) Sketch a drive system in which both pulleys have the same diameter. What is the angle of contact of the belt on the machine pulley?

(b) If the coefficient of friction, μ, is 0.4, what is the maximum value that the ratio T_T/T_S can reach before slipping will occur?

$$\frac{T_T}{T_S} = e^{\mu\theta}$$

and therefore

$$\ln\frac{T_T}{T_S} = \mu\theta$$

Answers to text questions

7.1 93 kW.
7.2 (a) $+2280$ N; (b) -2280 N.
7.4 85 N.
7.5 260 N.
7.6 (a) $180°$, or π rad; (b) 3.5.

8. Measuring temperature

Why measure temperature?

Figure 8.1 Two survey instruments on a tripod: an infrared distance meter and a theodolite. To obtain the correct distance, the atmospheric temperature must be known.

All properties of materials are temperature dependent; and the functioning of all physical, chemical and biological systems are temperature dependent.

The stability of insulation on electric wiring, and the stability of pn junctions in transistors, are dependent on temperature; each is destroyed if the temperature rises too high. The rates of chemical and biochemical reactions approximately double for a temperature rise of 10 K; and in the chemical industry the measurement and control of temperature in key places, such as reaction vessels, are of fundamental importance. Few industrial processes can be carried out without monitoring and controlling the temperature.

Figure 8.1 shows two survey instruments on a tripod. The upper instrument is a distance meter which directs an infrared laser beam on to a mirror at the distant spot, and measures the time of travel to the mirror and back. The speed of electromagnetic radiation in air depends upon the density of the air, which in turn depends upon its temperature. For distance measurements of over 100 m the air temperature has to be measured.

Figure 8.2 shows a resistance thermometer

Figure 8.2 A resistance thermometer probe inserted into pipework to measure the temperature of the fluid in the pipe. The measurement is then used to control the process. (Source: Matthey Electronics Limited.)

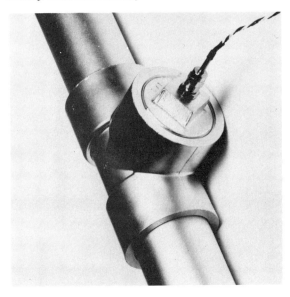

probe inserted into the flow path of a fluid in a pipe in a chemical plant. The results of temperature measurements are used to control the process, for instance by controlling the flow rate in the pipe, or by controlling the heating of the fluid elsewhere in the system.

Methods of measuring temperature

Any property of a material which changes in a regular way with temperature can be used to measure temperature. Broadly speaking, temperature measurements are based on four main types of physical change: expansion, electrical resistance, electrical contact potential (thermocouples), and electromagnetic radiation.

A change in the temperature of a substance produces a change in its length or volume, *expansion or contraction*; this is the basis of a wide range of thermometers: mercury in a glass, bimetallic, and constant pressure gas thermometers. If the material is constrained, and its volume is kept constant, then the pressure which it exerts changes. This is the basis of constant volume gas thermometers, and vapour pressure thermometers.

Figure 8.3 shows a bimetal thermometer being used to measure the temperature of setting concrete (a very important measurement in civil engineering, with regard to the later strength and reliability of the concrete). In order that the bimetallic strip may be accommodated inside the narrow tube of the steel stem, the strip is coiled into a helix. One end of the helix is anchored to the base of the stem; the other end is bent inwards on to the long axis of the helix, and is fitted with a spindle. When the temperature changes, the differential expansion and contraction of the bimetal strip in its helical form produces a rotary motion of the spindle. A pointer which moves over a graduated scale is attached to the spindle.

The *electrical resistance* of conductors and semiconductors changes with temperature. The metal conductors copper, nickel and platinum are used in resistance thermometry; thermistors, which are particularly temperature-sensitive semiconductors, are also used.

Where two dissimilar conductors are in contact there is a *contact potential*, and this is temperature dependent. This property enables the use of thermocouples as temperature measuring devices.

A hot body emits *electromagnetic radiation*. By measuring the effects of the radiation, the tempera-

Figure 8.3 *A bimetal thermometer and its principal parts. (a) A steel tube probe, sealed at the lower end, pushed into setting concrete. The bimetal is inside the sealed end.*
(b) From front to rear: a straight length of bimetal strip; coiled into a helix; helix fitted with a base for anchorage at one end, and a spindle at the other end; indicator needle; also a strip coiled into a flat spiral. (Parts supplied by British Rototherm Limited, Port Talbot.)

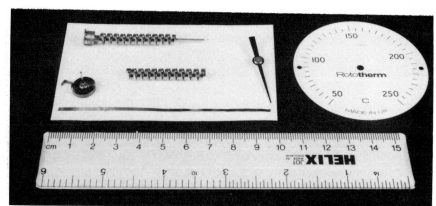

ture of the body may be determined. This is radiation pyrometry. It is the only method available when the object whose temperature is to be measured is so hot that it would damage an instrument in contact with it, for instance the interiors of some furnaces; and it is the only method available if the object is moving significantly. It is a *non-contact* method of determining temperature and is mainly used above about 1000 °C.

Temperature can only be measured by measuring the *change in a property* of a material *as its temperature changes*.

The primary fixed points

In order to give numerical values to temperature it is necessary to choose two situations which may be readily reproduced, and in which the temperature will always be the same. Arbitrary numerical values are then allocated to these two temperatures.

The readily reproducible situations which have been chosen are the *ice point* and the *steam point*. A mixture of pure ice and pure water in equilibrium with each other at standard atmospheric pressure constitutes the ice point, which is arbitrarily allotted the temperature of 0 °C. Pure water and steam (water vapour) in equilibrium with each other at standard atmospheric pressure constitutes the steam point, which is arbitrarily allotted the temperature of 100 °C.

The ice point and the steam point are the *primary fixed points*.

The fundamental interval

If the length of the mercury thread in a mercury in glass thermometer at the ice point is 30 mm, and its length at the steam point is 120 mm, then (120 mm − 30 mm) = 90 mm is known as the *fundamental interval* of the thermometer. It is the *change in length* of thread that represents a *change in temperature of 100 K*, in the region 0 °C to 100 °C.

If the change in thread length is proportional to the change in temperature, then by proportion:

Figure 8.4 *An unmarked mercury in glass thermometer at the ice point, the steam point, and at an unknown temperature, θ. The lengths of the mercury thread at these temperatures are l_0, l_{100}, and l_θ.*

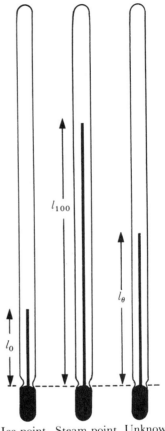

Ice point   Steam point   Unknown
0 °C   100 °C θ

$$\frac{\text{Temperature difference from ice point}}{100 \text{ K}}$$

$$= \frac{l_\theta - l_0}{l_{100} - l_0}$$

Temperature difference from ice point

$$= \frac{l_\theta - l_0}{l_{100} - l_0} \times 100 \text{ K}$$

As the ice point is defined as 0 °C on the celsius system, the temperature difference from the ice point gives the actual temperature in °C. Therefore

$$\theta = \frac{l_\theta - l_0}{l_{100} - l_0} \times 100 \text{ in } °C$$

In general, if the values of the thermometric property of a thermometer are X_0 at 0 °C, X_{100} at 100 °C and X_θ at an unknown temperature θ, then

$$\theta = \frac{X_\theta - X_0}{X_{100} - X_0} \times 100 \text{ in } °C \qquad (1)$$

This general equation when applied to particular types of thermometer becomes

Constant volume gas thermometer

$$\theta = \frac{p_\theta - p_0}{p_{100} - p_0} \times 100$$

Resistance thermometer

$$\theta = \frac{R_\theta - R_0}{R_{100} - R_0} \times 100$$

8.1 Figure 8.4 shows an unmarked thermometer drawn to its actual size. Its bulb and lower stem are at the ice point in (a), at the steam point in (b), and in a liquid of unknown temperature in (c).

(a) What is the fundamental interval of the thermometer?

(b) What is the temperature of the liquid?

A millimetre scale may be used to measure the thread lengths.

The general equation, equation (1), and those derived from it assume that the thermometric property which is being measured changes proportionally with change in temperature. This assumption is satisfactory for many purposes over a small temperature range, but it is in fact not true.

Scales of temperature

No substance has properties which change proportionally with temperature over a wide temperature range. Moreover, different substances depart from a linear relationship in different ways.

Thus if two different types of thermometer are each calibrated at the ice point and at the steam point, and if they are then put together in an oil bath, they will give different values for the temperature of the oil. A mercury in glass thermo-

meter might read 80.5 °C, and a resistance thermometer might give a value of 81.0 °C.

The type of thermometer which gives the most consistent results is the *constant volume gas thermometer*. Results using different gases in the bulb correlate well. At very low pressures, results are achieved which correspond to those which would be expected for an 'ideal gas'; and it has been possible to establish an *ideal gas scale* of temperature.

Around 1850, William Thomson, Professor of Physics at Glasgow University, examined ideas about heat engines that had been put forward by the French engineer Carnot. The efficiency of a heat engine depends upon its working temperature above absolute zero, and this enabled Thomson to produce a thermodynamic scale of temperature based on absolute zero. The absolute zero of temperature on Thomson's thermodynamic scale coincides with absolute zero on the ideal gas scale. Professor Thomson later became Lord Kelvin. The kelvin thermodynamic scale and the kelvin are named after him.

The *thermodynamic scale of temperature* is the *fundamental scale of temperature*. It is actually a theoretical scale, based on theoretical gas engines working without any real substance (no steam or gas). This raises the question of how it can be related to reality.

The thermodynamic scale can be achieved in practice by using the ideal gas scale, which involves the use of constant volume gas thermometers.

The *fundamental type of thermometer is the constant volume gas thermometer*.

Subsidiary fixed points

Precise measurements with gas thermometers are difficult to conduct and are very time-consuming. In normal work in laboratories, on machinery and in chemical plants, the types of thermometers needed are those which are simple to use and quick to provide a reading.

In addition to the fundamental fixed points of the ice point (0 °C and 273.15 K) and the steam point (100 °C and 373.15 K), subsidiary fixed points have been chosen. The temperatures of these

Figure 8.5 *Some internationally agreed subsidiary fixed points. The internationally agreed primary measuring instruments over three temperature ranges are also shown.*

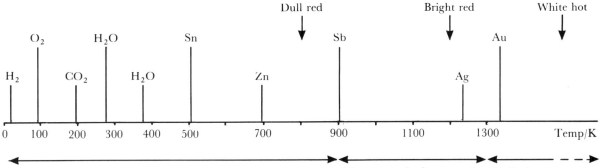

Platinum resistance thermometer

Thermocouple thermometer   Radiation pyrometer

have been measured accurately using constant volume gas thermometers, and they have been placed on the kelvin scale. These fixed points may be used to calibrate practical thermometers, such as resistance thermometers and thermocouples.

A selection of the subsidiary fixed points is shown in Figure 8.5, and some of the accurate temperature values are given in Table 8.1.

Table 8.1. *Some internationally agreed subsidiary fixed points*

Fixed point	bt of O_2	st of CO_2	ft of Sn	ft of Ag
Temperature (K)	90.188	194.670	505.118	1235.080

(bt, boiling temperature; st, subliming temperature; ft, freezing temperature)

In addition to some internationally agreed subsidiary fixed points, Figure 8.5 shows the internationally agreed types of thermometer for making reference measurements over three temperature ranges. Over the very wide range from about 20 K to about 900 K a precision platinum resistance thermometer is the standard instrument. From 900 K to 1300 K the standard is a thermocouple, one wire being platinum and the other an alloy of 10% rhodium and 90% platinum. Above 1300 K a radiation pyrometer is the reference instrument.

Each of these instruments is calibrated at two or more fixed points. The instruments can then be used to calibrate other types of thermometer. For instance, a bimetal thermometer manufactured for use between $-50\,^\circ\mathrm{C}$ and $-10\,^\circ\mathrm{C}$ could be calibrated by using a platinum resistance thermometer.

A high-precision platinum resistance thermometer

Figure 8.6 *A high-precision platinum resistance thermometer. Its overall length is about $\frac{1}{2}$ m and the stem diameter is about 7 mm. The resistance element is at the left-hand end, in the short white section, which is about 30 mm long. (Source: H. Tinsley and Company Limited, Croydon.)*

Platinum metal and resistance thermometry

Platinum resistance thermometers form the international reference standard for temperature measurement from $-260\,^\circ\mathrm{C}$ to $+850\,^\circ\mathrm{C}$. There are several reasons for this. The relationship between

Figure 8.7 *Temperature sensor in the form of a spiral of very fine platinum wire in a silica tube. Magnification, about 4×. (Source: H. Tinsley and Company.)*

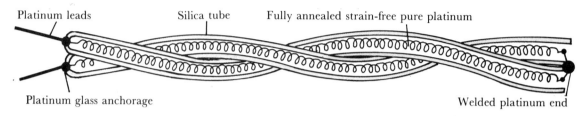

Platinum leads   Silica tube   Fully annealed strain-free pure platinum

Platinum glass anchorage   Welded platinum end

electrical resistance and temperature for pure platinum is very well defined, and over a considerable temperature range it is almost linear. The temperature coefficient of resistance, α, for platinum is among the highest available (α is the fractional change in resistance which results from a temperature change of 1 K). The metal can be refined to a very pure state; and it is very stable chemically. It is ductile and can readily be formed into a thin wire. Temperature determinations made using platinum wire resistors have high repeatability.

The structure of the thermometer

Figure 8.6 shows a high-precision platinum resistance thermometer. The stem is of quartz glass, about 7 mm in diameter and about $\frac{1}{2}$ m long. At the left-hand end in the short white section is the resistive element. It consists of a spiral of fine wire of pure platinum about 0.6 mm in diameter; the spiral is supported in two lengths of silica tube, slightly twisted on to each other.

Figure 8.7 shows the resistive element in more detail. The actual overall length of the twisted tubes is about 30 mm; the diagram has a magnification of about four.

The stem of the thermometer, and the silica tubes with the spirals, contain clean dry air at approximately $\frac{1}{3}$ atmospheric pressure at room temperature. This air is the main means of heat transfer between the outer quartz stem and the inner platinum spiral.

The leads from the spiral, up the inside stem to the head, are of thick platinum wire. In the head they are connected to two insulated copper conductors. The thick platinum leads are duplicated down

the length of the stem as far as the sensor, and in the head these duplicate leads are connected to a second pair of insulated copper conductors; together they form *compensating leads* whose function is described later in 'Measuring the resistance', p. 77.

The insulated copper conductors, in this instrument, end in spade terminals. Find the spade terminals in Figure 8.6 and confirm that there is a total of four leads from the instrument.

Specifications

The specifications given by the manufacturer are:

Temperature range	$-189\,°C$ to $+660\,°C$
Resistance at ice point	$25\,\Omega \pm 0.5\,\Omega$
Accuracy, over range $0\,°C$–$100\,°C$	$\pm 0.001\,°C$
Response time	10 to 15 s

The response time of a thermometer is the time it takes to reach 63% of the final temperature which it will record.

It is not necessary for each thermometer to have a particular resistance value at the ice point. Each thermometer will be calibrated at the ice point by having its resistance measured accurately, to ± 10 parts per million (that is, $\pm 0.001\%$). For convenience to users, the manufacturer guarantees that a thermometer's ice point resistance will lie between $24.5\,\Omega$ and $25.5\,\Omega$.

8.2 A precision thermometer's calibrations at the ice point and the steam point are:

$$R_0 = 25.2173\,\Omega, \text{ and } R_{100} = 35.1201\,\Omega.$$

What is the fundamental interval of that thermometer?

Measuring the resistance

Figure 8.8 *Two versions of the Wheatstone bridge circuit for measuring resistance. In (a), the resistor B is varied to bring the bridge into balance; in (b) the bridge is allowed to go out of balance, and the pd, V, across it is measured.*

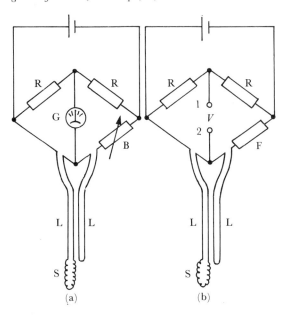

(a) (b)

In Figure 8.8(a) the thermometer with its leads is in one arm of the bridge. The compensating leads are in another arm together with a variable resistor, B. The other two arms contain resistors of equal value, R. The bridge will be in balance, with no deflection on the galvanometer, G, when the resistances of $(L+S) = (L+B)$. At that point, the resistance of the sensing element, S, equals the resistance of the variable resistor, B, and $S = B$.

In practice, instead of having a variable resistor, B, it is often more convenient to have a fixed resistor, F, and to allow the bridge to go out of balance. A potential difference then results across the bridge, between points 1 and 2, and this potential difference, V, is measured.

Calibrating the thermometer

High-precision platinum resistance thermometers such as the one that has been described are calibrated at the boiling point of oxygen, $-182.962\,°C$; the ice point;[1] the freezing point of

[1] The calibration is actually done at the 'triple point' of water, with ice, water, and water vapour in equilibrium, $0.010\,°C$.

Figure 8.9 *An industrial resistance bridge which will measure resistance to ± 2 parts per million. (Source: H. Tinsley and Company.)*

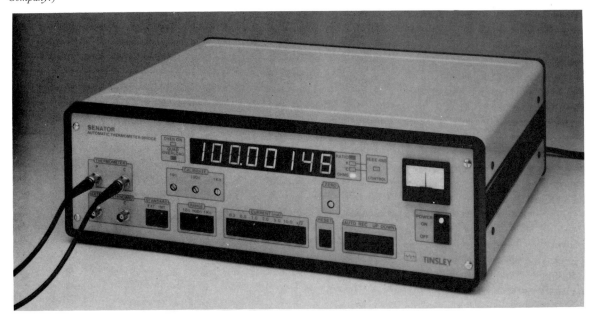

Figure 8.10 *High-precision platinum resistance thermometers being calibrated at the freezing points of tin and zinc. (Crown copyright. The National Physical Laboratory, Teddington.)*

tin, 231.968 °C; and the freezing point of zinc, 419.580 °C. Figure 8.10 shows a calibration being performed at the National Physical Laboratory, which provides a calibration service. Inside the cabinet, a pure metal is contained in a pure graphite crucible, and this is encapsulated in a long argon-filled silica tube. The whole is heated in a cylindrical furnace to approximately 10 K above the melting temperature. A slow, controlled cooling period follows until the freezing-point equilibrium is reached. Readings are then taken.

Calibration uncertainties for high-precision platinum resistance thermometers (Class 1) are shown in Table 8.2.

Table 8.2. Calibration uncertainties for high-precision (Class 1) platinum resistance thermometers at various temperatures.

Temperature (°C)	−183	0	100	400
Uncertainty (K)	±0.003	±0.001	±0.001	±0.002

(*Source:* National Physical Laboratory, Teddington.)

Usage and use

The manufacturer's instructions include the following sentences: 'After calibration the thermometer must be handled very carefully to retain its calibration characteristics. When not in use the thermometer should be kept in the special case provided for it.'

The principal use of this precision thermometer is for calibrating other types of thermometer.

A good-quality, low-cost resistance thermometer

Figure 8.11 *An industrial resistance thermometer. (a) Actual size. (b) Magnified to 3× actual size. The sensor consists of a platinum film track on a ceramic tile. (Sample supplied by Matthey Electronics Limited.)*

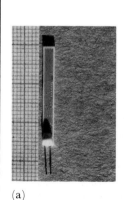

(a)

(b)

The sensor

For most industrial uses, a thermometer needs to have a sensor which is *sturdy*, which will *stand movement* from place to place, and which will *stand vibration* when it is in place in use. It should also be *inexpensive*.

A resistance thermometer sensor which meets these needs is shown in Figure 8.11. It consists of a platinum film track laid down on a ceramic tile support. The platinum track is covered by a thin glass glaze, to protect it. Double, electrically parallel, loops in the track can be cut by a laser beam to adjust the effective length of track, and thus adjust the resistance to the required value. (The manufacture of this sensor is described in detail in the companion volume *Electricity*.)

The manufacturer provides three grades of this sensor, Grades A, B and C. Most users find that for their purposes, for instance for process control in a chemical plant, a Grade B sensor is very suitable. In this, the resistance at the ice point is $100.00 \, \Omega \pm 0.12 \, \Omega$, representing a temperature uncertainty of $\pm 0.3 \, ^\circ\text{C}$. The sensor is suitable for measurements in the temperature range $-70 \, ^\circ\text{C}$ to $+600 \, ^\circ\text{C}$.

The fundamental interval

Figure 8.12 *Platinum resistance sensors being measured for their resistance at the ice point and at the steam point. (Matthey Electronics Limited.)*

The design *fundamental interval* for these resistance sensors is $38.50 \, \Omega$. That is, if the resistance of a sensor is $100.00 \, \Omega$ at the ice point, the design intention is that it should be $138.50 \, \Omega$ at the steam point.

The photograph in Figure 8.12 shows the resistance of sensors being measured at the steam point and at the ice point. In the foreground, the large cylindrical tank is the steam bath. The vertical thin tubes are probes, each having a sensor at the bottom in the steam bath. Each sensor is connected to a computer. When the resistance has stabilised at the steam point, the resistance value is recorded. The process is then repeated in an ice/water bath, which is situated beyond the steam bath on the operator's right. For each sensor, the computer then calculates its fundamental interval and its temperature coefficient of resistance, α. Each sensor is then placed in bins according to categories of Grades A, B and C.

To be accepted as a Grade B sensor, the ice point resistance must be within $0.12 \, \Omega$ of the design resistance of $100.00 \, \Omega$. That is, its resistance must be between $99.88 \, \Omega$ and $100.12 \, \Omega$, which represents a temperature uncertainty of $\pm 0.3 \, ^\circ\text{C}$. Also, the fundamental interval (FI) must be within $0.12 \, \Omega$ of the design FI of $38.50 \, \Omega$; that is, the FI must be between $38.38 \, \Omega$ and $38.62 \, \Omega$.

For most industrial purposes, a Grade B sensor is very satisfactory.

8.3 Examine Table 8.3, and read the caption. Select any one sensor and confirm that it is within the limits set by the company for a Grade

	Resistance (Ω)	
Sensor no.	Ice point	Steam point
1	99.92	138.45
2	99.89	138.40
3	100.04	138.60
4	100.03	138.62

(*Source:* Matthey Electronics Limited.)

Table 8.3. Extract from a calibration certificate for sensors of the type given in Figure 8.11. It is provided by the manufacturer for a customer

B sensor. That is, confirm that the freezing point resistance, and the fundamental interval, lie within the limits given on page 79.

Making measurements

The sensor is used in a Wheatstone bridge circuit, using compensating leads, as was shown in Figure 8.8. The equal resistances, R, are $4000\,\Omega$ each. The resistance B should be variable on either side of $100\,\Omega$; and the resistance F should be $100.00\,\Omega$. A power supply of $12\,V$ is suitable.

The most convenient method of obtaining a temperature value is to use the circuit shown in Figure 8.9(b), and to measure the potential difference, V, across the bridge (terminals 1 and 2) when the bridge is unbalanced. A high-resistance voltmeter would be used. Taking the resistance values for R and F that were given in the preceding paragraph, $1\,mV$ represents $1\,K$ above or below $0.0\,°C$.

Resistance tolerance and temperature uncertainty

The resistance tolerance changes with temperature, and thus the temperature uncertainty also changes. A Grade B sensor would operate within the limits shown in Table 8.4.

Table 8.4. Resistance tolerance and temperature uncertainty at various temperatures

Temperature (°C)	−100	0	100	200	300	400
Resistance tolerance ($\pm\Omega$)		0.2	0.1	0.2	0.35	0.5	0.65
Temperature uncertainty ($\pm°C$)		0.5	0.3	0.5	1.0	1.4	1.9

(*Source:* Matthey Electronics Limited.)

Some uses of the sensor

Figure 8.13 shows some ways in which a good-quality, low-cost platinum film sensor may be used to measure temperature. Of the many different fields of use for the sensor, the principal one is in

Figure 8.13 *Some uses of platinum film resistance sensors in measuring temperature. (a) A thermometer probe ($\frac{1}{3}$ size) for inserting into pipelines and chemical reactor vessels, for process control. (b) A cut-away section of a cylinder for lowering into oil well drillings.*

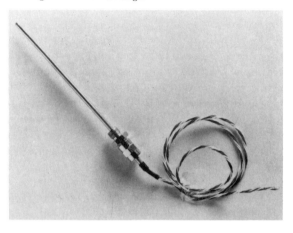

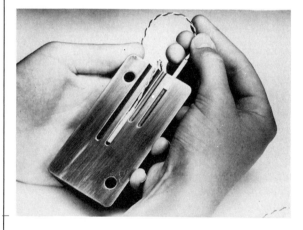

process control: the sensing of temperature and temperature change, and feeding this information to a controlling mechanism.

Figure 8.14 shows a resistance thermometer being used to control the temperature in a chemical reaction vessel. Examine the diagram, and note how the control is achieved.

Answers to text questions

8.1 (a) 50 mm; (b) 40 °C.
8.2 9.9028 Ω.

Figure 8.13 cont. *(c) Measurement of the surface temperature of pipes. (d) Measurement of the temperature of the air around the components on printed circuit boards. (Source: Matthey Electronics Limited.)*

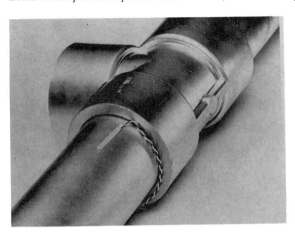
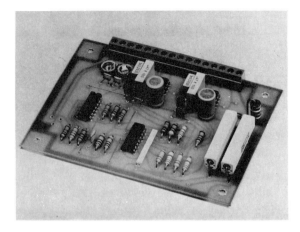

Figure 8.14 *Mixture of liquid reactants in a reaction vessel and a means of maintaining the temperature of the reactants close to a chosen value.*

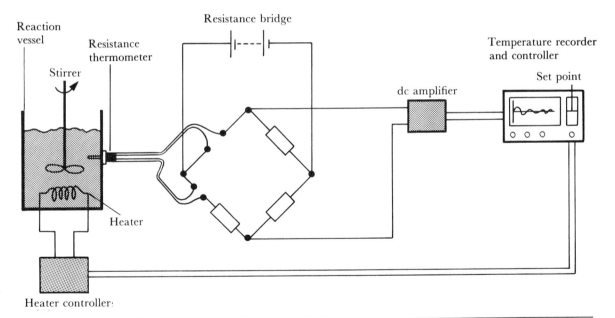

9. Heat: its nature and relevance

What is heat?

Heat is energy in transit due to a temperature difference

Wherever there is a temperature difference in a medium, or between two media, energy will flow from the place at the higher temperature to the place at the lower temperature. *Heat is a flow process*; it is a transport process.

If the quantity of energy transferred is measured in joules, and if the time for the transfer to take place is measured in seconds, then the rate of energy transfer as heat is in joules per second or watts.

There are three modes of energy transfer as heat; these are *conduction*, *convection*, and *radiation*. Their mechanisms and their rate equations are considered later in this chapter.

In many fields of engineering, the design of a system is dominated by heat considerations. In the design of large electric motors, large alternators and large transformers a means must be provided for the removal of the very large quantities of energy which are released by the current in the coils, at the rate of $I^2 R$ joules per second, and cooling arrangements have to be designed into the system. All engineers find that their work includes heat processes, either because they wish to transfer energy as heat or because the process produces heat and the energy has to be removed from the system.

This very wide-ranging importance of heat, of energy flow, in engineering is now considered.

The importance of heat in engineering

Heating

Heating involves transferring energy to the substance which is being processed, with a resultant

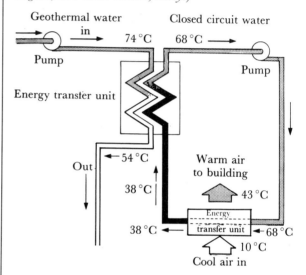

Figure 9.1 *Warm air for space heating in a building being produced from geothermal hot water. (Adapted from a diagram, APV Baker Limited, Derby.)*

rise in its temperature. Heating by means of furnaces is needed in the production and subsequent treatment of metals; and it is needed in the production of hot water and steam for industrial processes. Heating is required for many chemical reactions, and for distillation and for evaporation. The energy required may be provided in many ways: by means of combustion in a furnace, by steam, by hot water or other hot fluid, or by electrical heating.

Figure 9.1 shows geothermal hot water being used to heat cool air from outside a building in order to produce warm air for use inside the building. The heating is done in two stages by means of two energy transfer units. One reason for this is that the geothermal water is obtained from deep wells and thus contains dissolved salts which are corrosive, so that the water cannot be passed direct round the heating system of the building.

Instead, it enters the building through cast iron pipes, and then through passages made from stainless steel in an energy transfer unit, where it is in close proximity to cool water being pumped past it.

Examine Figure 9.1. The cool water is heated by the geothermal water, and this heated water is pumped round a closed circuit system to another energy transfer unit where incoming cool air is warmed by it. The warmed air is then passed to the building spaces.

Cooling

Figure 9.2 *A mobile generator of alternating current. The eight-cylinder diesel engine can transmit 270 kW of power along the shaft to the alternator. Cooling of the cylinder by water absorbs about 150 kW of power, and this has to be transferred to the atmosphere through the energy transfer unit on the left. (Source: Tripower Limited.)*

Cooling involves transferring energy away from the substance being processed, with a resultant drop in its temperature.

Where the temperature of a substance or a system has to be lowered and maintained at a temperature which is below that of the surrounding atmosphere, the process is called *refrigeration*; refrigeration processes are widespread and important.

Far more widespread in engineering are circumstances in which a system releases or transforms energy, which results in a rise in the temperature of part of the system. The temperature rise might become so great that part of the system could become damaged, and in that case the temperature rise would have to be controlled by the removal of energy, that is, by cooling.

Combustion processes release energy, resulting in high temperatures in combustion chambers. An electric current in a conductor releases energy at a rate of I^2R joules per second, where I is the current in amps and R is the resistance of the conductor in ohms; this raises the temperature of the conductor. A rise in temperature is an inevitable consequence when a conductor or an electrical component carries a current; and in most electrical machines, devices and systems the temperature rise and operating temperature have to be calculated; and the temperature rise may have to be limited by providing a cooling system.

Figure 9.2 shows an ac generator. The engine is an eight-cylinder diesel, and combustion in its cylinders releases energy at the rate of $750 \, \text{kJ s}^{-1}$, that is, 750 kW. But of this, only about 36% can be converted into useful power, so that the power which is transmitted along the shaft to the alternator (dynamo) is only 270 kW. The balance, that is $(750 \, \text{kW} - 270 \, \text{kW})$, or 480 kW, is removed to the surroundings in various ways. The cooling water which flows around the hot cylinders removes about $150 \, \text{kJ s}^{-1}$, raising the temperature of the water to over $90 \, ^\circ\text{C}$. Before this water can be recycled it has to be cooled, which is the function of the large 'radiator' mounted on the left of the engine. It must transfer $150 \, \text{kJ s}^{-1}$ to the atmosphere, that is, 150 kW; it does this almost entirely by forced convection. (For this reason the term 'radiator' is inappropriate for the unit.)

The temperature of the burned gases in the cylinder of an internal combustion engine can be at about $2000 \, ^\circ\text{C}$. The cylinders and cylinder heads are made of metals or alloys whose strengths begin to decrease above about $200 \, ^\circ\text{C}$. Therefore a cooling system is needed for the cylinders and cylinder heads to keep their temperature below about $200 \, ^\circ\text{C}$. Some engines are air-cooled and some are water-cooled.

Figure 9.3(a) shows the water cooling route by which energy is removed from the high-

Figure 9.3 *The principles of water cooling and oil cooling in internal combustion engines. Energy from high-temperature burned gases is removed: by conduction through metal walls; by convection in fluids; and by radiation from the sump case.*

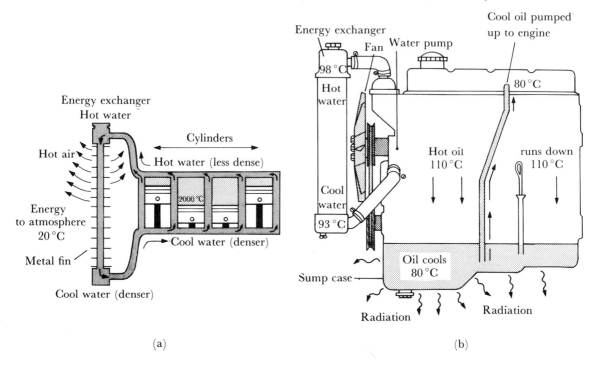

(a)   (b)

temperature gases in the cylinders in a water-cooled engine: by *conduction* through the cylinders' metal walls, and by *convection* in the water system; by *conduction* through the copper walls of the water cooler, and by *convection* into the atmosphere. The hot lubricating oil loses energy to the atmosphere mainly by *radiation* from the sump case, and this is shown in Figure 9.3(b).

Figure 9.3(b) also shows that in most four-cylinder engines the circulation of water by convection is aided by a water pump; and the flow of air to cool the water is aided by a fan. Each of these is an example of *forced convection*. A typical temperature difference between the hot water at the top of the energy exchanger and the cool water at its foot is about 5 K.

Look again at Figure 9.2 and examine the water cooling system: look at the size of the energy exchanger, and look for the hot water inlet and cool water outlet.

Also, look again at the photograph of the excavator given in Figure 5.3. This has a six-

cylinder diesel engine which provides 44 kW of working power, representing 35% efficiency in conversion of fuel to work. Locate the engine 'radiator' grille.

Table 9.1 shows by percentages the ways in which energy from combustion of diesel fuel in the cylinders is used and lost.

On the generator shown in Figure 9.2, the alternator is at the right-hand end; note how small it is compared with the engine which drives it. The inspector is working at the alternator. At the left-hand end of the alternator is a series of horizontal louvres, or openings, one above the other. These are air inlets to allow a fan to draw cooling air over the rotor coils and stator coils of the alternator, and to maintain them at a temperature at which they will not become damaged.

The drive shaft from the engine delivers 270 kW of mechanical power to the alternator, and the alternator can provide 250 kW of electrical power. Most of the 20 kW loss occurs in the form of I^2R loss from the currents in the coils of the alternator; and

Table 9.1. Power information for the six-cylinder diesel engine in the excavator shown in Figure 5.3, at an engine speed of 1500 rev min^{-1}

Combustion of fuel (kW)	Useful power (kW)	Where the energy goes				
		Useful work (%)	Cooling water (%)	Exhaust (%)	Radiation (%)	Total (%)
125	44	35	20	36	9	100

(*Source:* Ford Motor Company, Dagenham.)

this raises the temperature of the coils. If the temperature rises too high the insulation on the conductors in the windings will become damaged; and the operating temperature of the coils is kept down at about 120 °C (about 100 K above atmospheric temperature) by the flow of cooling air. The cooling air has to remove energy at a rate of 20 kJ per second, that is 20 kW.

In power supply and in power conversion, alternators, transformers and electric motors have to be designed with cooling as a prime consideration; and they have to be provided with appropriate cooling arrangements.

One of the main causes of failure of power semiconductors is in allowing the pn junctions to reach too high a temperature. Germanium devices can operate up to a limit of about 100 °C, and

silicon devices up to a limit of about 175 °C. Above these temperatures, the junctions begin to disintegrate. Manufacturers of semiconductor devices provide data sheets for their products which give the maximum recommended operating temperature for the junction.

The forward voltage drop across the junction, and the conduction current, result in an I^2R power loss in the junction region; and the energy which is released raises the temperature of the junction. The energy must be removed at a sufficient rate to prevent the junction temperature from rising too high; for this purpose the casing of the semiconductor may be fixed to a cooling device formed from a metal structure with a large surface area. Energy from the junction region is then removed through the device's body by conduction, along the metal structure by conduction, and into the surrounding air by convection and radiation.

The photograph in Figure 9.4 shows a number of such cooling devices, termed *heatsinks*. They have fins to give a large surface area in a small volume; they are mounted vertically to allow the best development of air convection currents; and they are painted black to make a good radiator surface.

Insulating

When *thermal insulation* is placed in a heat path it *reduces the rate at which energy is transferred.*

Thermal insulation can be used to keep a substance or a place cool in relation to its surroundings. Ice may be kept in a vacuum flask on a summer day when the surroundings are at 20 °C or

Figure 9.4 A power supply unit for converting ac into very high grade dc. It contains several heat sinks, the black devices with vertical fins, which are used to cool power diodes and power transistors. (Source: Coden Electronics Limited, Hitchin.)

Figure 9.5 *(a) A large-diameter insulated pipe at an oil installation. (b) The insulation material and its aluminium sheet cover. (Source: The Chemical and Insulating Company Limited, Darlington.)*

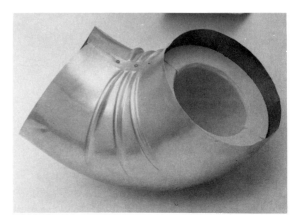

30 °C. In a top-floor room on a sunny summer day, if there is a good thickness of insulation above the ceiling, the room may remain cool relative to the high temperature in the roof space, which is heated by the hot roof. In each case a flow of energy has been limited or restricted by the insulation. An *inflow* of energy has been restricted in order to restrict a rise in temperature.

Most of the uses of thermal insulation, however, are to reduce an *outflow* of energy from a system, in order to reduce the loss of energy and to reduce the fall in temperature of the system.

In the manufacture of chemicals in chemical plant, in the distillation of oil in refineries, and in the production of electricity in power stations, it is necessary to convey large quantities of very hot fluids along pipes. And it is often necessary for the temperature of the fluids to remain high. If bare pipes were used the energy losses would be large and thus the temperature drops in the materials would be large. The pipes need insulation to reduce the rate at which energy is lost and thus to reduce the rate at which the temperature drops.

Figure 9.5(a) shows a large-diameter insulated pipe at an oil installation. (b) shows the insulation for such a pipe, enclosed in its cover of aluminium sheet. The insulation material is specially prepared

calcium silicate, which is stable at high temperatures and can be used up to 700 °C, at which temperature it will be red hot.

Figure 9.6 represents (actual size) a pipe containing a red hot fluid at 650 °C. The insulation material is chosen to withstand this temperature; and its thickness is chosen so as to reduce the rate of energy loss to an acceptable value, and to provide at the outside, at the aluminium cover, a temperature which is low enough not to endanger any person who accidentally touches the cover.

Unnecessary loss of energy involves waste of fuel. This involves unnecessary atmospheric pollution and waste of money. Table 9.2 shows the loss of energy, in terms of tonnes of heating oil, which

Table 9.2. The energy loss per year along a 100 m length of an uninsulated pipe of the size of that shown in Figure 9.6. The energy loss is given in terms of tonnes of heating oil per year.

Temperature of pipe and contents	100 °C	300 °C
Loss of energy, in tonnes of fuel oil	30 t	200 t

(*Source:* Derived from data from The Chemical and Insulating Company.)

Figure 9.6 *Life size representation of a pipe containing fluid at 650 °C and its insulation of specially prepared calcium silicate.*

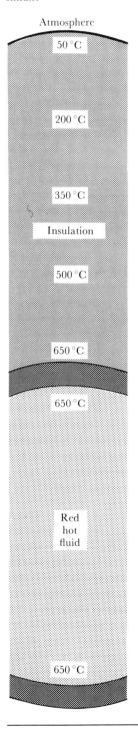

occurs in a year along 100 m of uninsulated pipe of the size shown in Figure 9.6 (but with much cooler fluids in the pipe than the 650 °C mentioned above).

Within the chemical industry, 100 °C is not a high temperature for the contents of a pipe, and 100 m is not a long length. Yet in such circumstances energy to the equivalent of 30 t of heating oil would be wasted per year; and the figure would be 200 t per year if the fluid and the pipe were at 300 °C. For materials which have to be kept hot, efficient insulation of their containers is essential in economic terms and is very important in environmental terms.

Recovering energy

In order to raise the temperature of a material, energy has to be provided; this requires fuel and therefore money. From the commercial and industrial aspects, energy which remains unused at the end of the process need not be totally wasted; much of it may be used for heating purposes, by using a suitable energy exchanger. This is termed *energy recovery*.

For instance, in large commercial dishwashers, such as those used in hotels and restaurants, the waste water may leave the dishwasher at about 60 °C. Incoming water from the mains, with a temperature of about 10 °C, will be relatively cold; thus the relatively hot dishwasher effluent can be used to heat up the mains inflow, raising its temperature before it goes to the water heater. In this way, both fuel and money are saved. Using a suitable energy exchanger, the cost of the exchanger and its installation may be recovered from energy savings in about three months; and in about three years the savings may cover the costs of the dishwashers themselves.

Figure 9.7 illustrates an energy recovery system using an energy exchanger. Select some point in the flow, for instance the operations in the top part of the diagram, and follow the system round to see how energy that would otherwise be wasted is recovered and used.

Swimming baths provide another example. 'Bleed-off water' from the pool can be used to raise

Figure 9.7 *Warm waste water from washing and other processes being passed through an energy exchanger, where it warms incoming cold mains water. (Adapted from a diagram, BSS Industrial Heating and Pipeline Supplies Limited, Leicester.)*

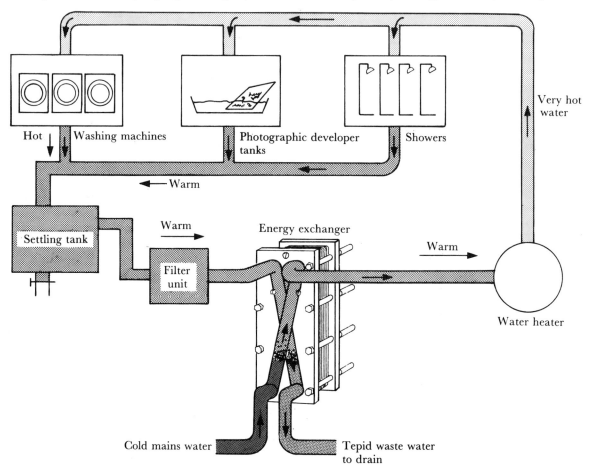

the temperature of incoming water; and waste water from the showers may be used to heat up water which is on its way to the main water heater. In a typical swimming pool complex with a 1000 m³ pool it is possible to save about 100 t of fuel oil each year by these means.

Figure 9.8 shows part of a chemical plant. In one stage, a solution of sodium hydroxide at a temperature of 75 °C has to be cooled to 31 °C. This is done with cool water from a cooling tower, and in the course of the operation the temperature of the water becomes raised to over 60 °C. This hot water is not wasted; it is used to raise the temperature of incoming river water, which needs to be hot for another part of the process.

Examine Figure 9.8. Look at the temperature changes in the liquids in energy exchanger A. Look at the change in the temperature of the river water as it passes through energy exchanger B. Find part of the system which forms a cycle.

Figure 9.8 *Two energy recovery stages in a chemical plant. The temperatures are in* °C. *(Adapted from a diagram, APV Baker Limited, Derby.)*

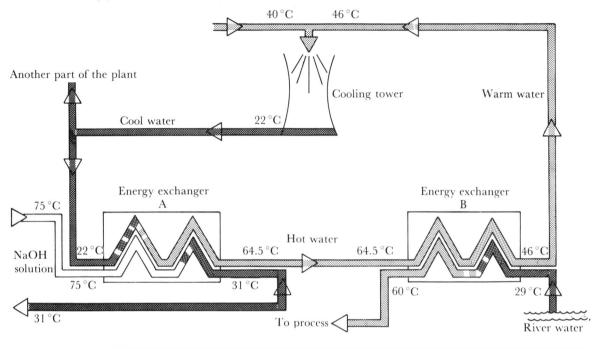

10. Heat modes and heat rates

Introduction

Heat is energy in transit due to a temperature difference; there are three modes by which it may occur: *conduction*; *convection*; and *radiation*.

In most practical situations, energy is transported by at least two of these modes in conjunction, and very often by all three of them in conjunction. In order to design machinery and equipment, and in order to control them and the processes within them, it is necessary to know the *modes* by which energy is transferred as a result of temperature differences; and it is necessary to be able to calculate the *rates* at which the energy may be transferred.

Conduction

Conduction takes place in the course of transfer of energy from more energetic particles to less energetic ones by interaction between them. Lattice vibrations are more vigorous on the higher-temperature side of a solid than on the lower-temperature side, and the more vigorous vibrations pass energy through the lattice in the form of lattice waves towards the lower-temperature side.

If the material contains free electrons (mobile electrons) these move about more rapidly in a higher-temperature region than in a lower-temperature one, and in their random movement they transfer energy towards the lower-temperature region.

Materials that have no mobile electrons can transfer thermal energy by lattice waves only. Materials that have mobile electrons, for instance metals, can transfer thermal energy both by lattice vibration waves and by electron migration. Thus metals are good conductors of both thermal energy and electricity.

Figure 10.1(a) illustrates this. The diagram shows a block of solid material, with the left-hand face at a higher temperature, θ_1, than the right-hand face, θ_2. Vigorous lattice vibrations at the left-hand side of the block are creating lattice vibration waves through the block, and energy is flowing from left to right.

If the energy which flows through some area of the face is ΔQ joules in a time of Δt seconds, then

$$\text{Energy flow rate} = \frac{\Delta Q}{\Delta t} \quad (\text{J s}^{-1} \text{ or W})$$

Figure 10.1(b) shows how the temperature changes with distance across the block; and it shows the slope of the graph, the *temperature gradient*, $-\Delta\theta/\Delta x$. The sign is negative because the slope is negative; the temperature, θ, decreases as the distance, x, increases.

It can be found experimentally that the energy flow rate is proportional to *the area* of the face, and to the temperature gradient:

$$\frac{\Delta Q}{\Delta t} \propto A; \text{ and } \frac{\Delta Q}{\Delta t} \propto -\frac{\Delta\theta}{\Delta x}$$

Therefore

$$\frac{\Delta Q}{\Delta t} = -kA\frac{\Delta\theta}{\Delta x} \tag{1}$$

The *proportionality constant* k is called the *thermal conductivity* of the substance.

In order to find the units of k (thermal conductivity), we may rearrange equation (1):

$$-\frac{\Delta Q}{\Delta t} \times \frac{1}{A} \times \frac{\Delta x}{\Delta\theta} = k$$

and the units are

$$\text{J} \times \text{s}^{-1} \times \text{m}^{-2} \times \text{m} \times \text{K}^{-1} = \text{W m}^{-1}\text{K}^{-1}$$

Table 10.1 gives the thermal conductivity of some materials. Copper and aluminium are excellent conductors of heat and of electricity. The

Figure 10.1 *(a) Energy flowing through a solid block as a result of a temperature difference between its faces, a high temperature θ_1 on the left and a lower temperature θ_2 on the right. (b) This graph shows how the temperature changes with distance across the block.*

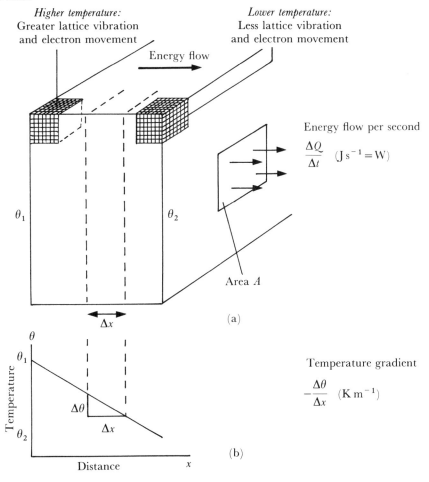

Table 10.1. The thermal conductivity k $(\mathrm{W\,m^{-1}\,K^{-1}})$ of some solid materials, at $27\,^\circ\mathrm{C}$

Elements		Other materials						
		Domestic (structural)		Foodstuffs		Fluids		Insulation	
Cu	400	Glass	1.4	Chicken meat	0.5	Water	0.61	Cork	0.04
Al	240	Common brick	0.72	Apple	0.5	Engine oil	0.14	Glass fibre[a]	0.04
Fe	80	Soft wood	0.35	Cake batter	0.2	Air	0.026	Polystyrene[b]	0.03
S	0.2								

Notes:

(a) In blanket form.

(b) Expanded polystyrene in board form.

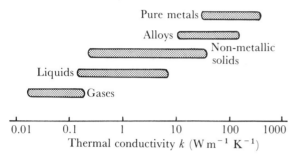

Figure 10.2 *The approximate ranges of thermal conductivity values for five classes of materials.*

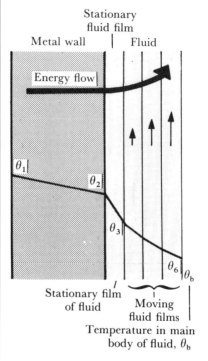

Figure 10.3 *A hot metal wall with cooler fluid on one side. The fluid film in contact with the wall and very close to it is stationary. The temperature profile is shown, dropping from θ_1 to θ_6, and θ_b in the main body of the fluid.*

mobile, free electrons are responsible. Sulphur is a non-metal; its lattice structure has no mobile electrons, and its thermal conductivity is low.

The thermal conductivity of foodstuffs is low. When cold food is heated in a gas or electric oven energy travels only slowly from the hot outside of the food to the cold inside.

Fluids may be stationary, for instance the thin film of oil or water adjacent to the wall of its container. Small pockets of trapped air, as in cotton wool, may also be stationary. These have low values of conductivity.

Examine the diagram in Figure 10.2. If energy is to be transferred from one place to another by conduction, then a suitable metal or alloy will be the transfer medium to choose if at all possible.

Convection

Convection is energy transfer *between a surface and a fluid moving over the surface.* It is made up of three basic processes. First, there is a *stationary film* of fluid next to the surface, and energy transfer through this can only take place by *conduction*. This is shown in Figure 10.3, where at the metal wall's inner surface the temperature is θ_2 and drops through the stationary film to θ_3.

Second, beyond the stationary film, fluid moves with increasing speed until a steady speed is reached in the bulk of the fluid. Molecules at the stationary film boundary have a temperature of θ_3 and possess greater energy than those with lower temperatures nearer the bulk of the fluid. They

move by *diffusion* into the bulk of the fluid carrying energy with them and transferring some of it to molecules which are at a lower temperature, θ_4, θ_5 and θ_6.

Third, the temperature of the body of the fluid rises; its density decreases; and a buoyancy effect occurs. As a result of this, the warmed fluid rises and *bulk motion* conveys energy away.

The three main processes are thus *conduction* through the stationary film of fluid; *diffusion* of energetic molecules into the less energetic bulk; and *bulk motion* of the fluid due to a reduced density leading to buoyancy.

The process which has just been described is *natural convection*, and it will take place where fluids can rise past heated surfaces. The rate of energy transfer can be increased by forcing the fluid to travel faster than by the usually rather slow natural convection, and this can be achieved by employing fans for gases and pumps for fluids. This is called *forced convection*. Examples of forced convection are shown in Figure 9.3(b) in an internal combustion engine cooling system, and in Figure 13.3 in the cooling of a heat sink for a power transistor.

The *energy flow rate*, $\Delta Q / \Delta t$, from a surface into a fluid by convection is proportional to the area of the surface, A, and to the temperature difference between the surface and the main body of the fluid, $(\theta_s - \theta_b)$.

$$\frac{\Delta Q}{\Delta t} \propto A(\theta_s - \theta_b)$$

This is Newton's Law of Cooling. If ΔQ, the energy transferred, is in joules and if Δt, the time taken, is in seconds then $\Delta Q / \Delta t$ is in $J\,s^{-1}$ or W:

$$\frac{\Delta Q}{\Delta t} = hA(\theta_s - \theta_b) \tag{2}$$

The proportionality factor, h, is known as the *convection energy transfer coefficient* (and sometimes as the *film coefficient*, which emphasises the importance of the stationary film). By rearranging equation (2) to give h, its units can be shown to be $W\,m^{-2}\,K^{-1}$.

Table 10.2. *Typical values of the convection energy transfer coefficient, h ($W\,m^{-2}\,K^{-1}$)*

Free convection	Forced convection	Boiling and condensing
Gases 2–25	Gases 25–250	Phase change
Liquids 50–1000	Liquids 50–20 000	2500–100 000

10.1 *Convection heating.* A room is heated by a bare steam pipe. The room temperature is 27 °C and the temperature of the surface of the pipe is 127 °C. The pipe is 15 m long and has an external diameter of 70 mm. The convection energy transfer coefficient is $h = 15\,W\,m^{-2}\,K^{-1}$. (a) At what rate is the pipe transferring energy into the room by convection? (b) By what other mode will the pipe be heating the room significantly?

The behaviour of fluids in convection and obtaining a value for the coefficient h is of great importance in the design of energy exchangers and in their functioning. Some types of energy exchangers are considered in Chapter 11.

Radiation

Thermal radiation is emitted by all forms of matter which are above the absolute zero of temperature. The energy comes from an electron in an atom falling from one energy level to another, emitting a photon; and the energy is transported by electromagnetic waves. Conduction and convection require a medium by which to transport energy; but electromagnetic radiation can travel through a vacuum, and can transport energy through empty space.

The rate at which the surface of a body radiates energy is proportional to the *surface area*, A, of the body, and to the *fourth power of its thermodynamic temperature (absolute temperature)*, T^4:

$$\frac{\Delta Q}{\Delta t} \propto A T^4$$

The proportionality constant is the Stephan–Boltzmann constant, σ (which has the value $\sigma = 5.7 \times 10^{-8}\,W\,m^{-2}\,K^{-4}$).

For an ideal radiator (a pure black body)

$$\frac{\Delta Q}{\Delta t} = \sigma A T^4$$

For a real body

$$\frac{\Delta Q}{\Delta t} = \varepsilon \sigma A T^4 \tag{3}$$

No real body or surface is an ideal radiator; and the extent to which it departs from or approaches ideal behaviour is indicated by its emissivity, ε, which can range from almost 0 for a very poor radiator to almost 1 for a near ideal radiator.

For instance, values of ε at a temperature of 300 °C are: copper, highly polished 0.04, oxidised 0.5; and stainless steel, polished 0.2, oxidised 0.7. At

Figure 10.4 *Values for the emissivity of different types of materials.*

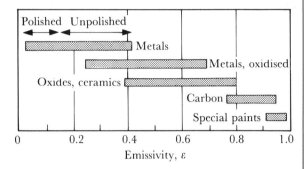

27 °C, values of ε are: red house brick, 0.95; skin, vegetation and water, about 0.95; and a special black paint, 0.98.

Examine Figure 10.4, and note that highly polished metals have very low emissivities; a layer of metal oxide raises the emissivity, often very greatly, and specially prepared paints can have very high values.

A body *radiates energy* as a consequence of its own temperature; it also *receives energy* falling on it as radiation *from the surroundings*. This is shown in Figure 10.5, where a steam pipe is heating a room. The pipe, at 127 °C, radiates energy to the room: to

Figure 10.5 *A hot pipe in a room. The pipe radiates energy; it also receives energy radiated by the room. (T_s, temperature of the surface of the steam pipe, 127°C; T_{sur}, temperature of the surrounding room, 27°C).*

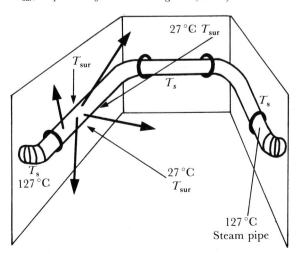

the walls, the ceiling and the floor. The pipe also receives radiant energy from the walls, ceiling and floor at 27 °C. Under the circumstances

Net energy radiated by pipe = total energy radiated by pipe − radiant energy absorbed from surroundings

For very many situations this can be represented by the equation

$$\frac{\Delta Q}{\Delta t} = \varepsilon \sigma A (T_s^4 - T_{sur}^4) \qquad (4)$$

This equation is derived from equation (3); A is the area of the surface of the pipe, and ε is its emissivity. Thus for the room in Figure 10.5, the net rate at which energy is being radiated by the pipe into the room is

$$\frac{\Delta Q}{\Delta t} = \varepsilon \sigma A (400^4 - 300^4)$$

where the temperatures are on the absolute scale, in kelvin.

10.2 *Net rate of radiant energy transfer to a room.* Examine the room and pipe shown in Figure 10.5. The pipe is 15 m long and has an external diameter of 70 mm. The emissivity of the surface of the pipe is $\varepsilon = 0.8$, and the value of the constant σ is $\sigma = 5.7 \times 10^{-8}\ \mathrm{W\,m^{-2}\,K^{-4}}$.

(a) Calculate the net rate at which the pipe is radiating energy into the room.

(b) The pipe is the same as that in Question 10.1. Using your answer to the convection heating in Question 10.1, show the contribution in kilowatts which the pipe makes to heating the room (i) by convection; (ii) by radiation; and (iii) the combination.

Transformer cooling: conduction, convection and radiation

Most engineering systems experience thermal energy transfer through all the three modes at once. Electric motors, alternators, and transformers have energy released in their windings as a result of I^2R

Figure 10.6 *A winding being made for a large transformer. Horizontal strips of compressed fibre board separate the windings from the cylinder and create channels along which cooling oil may flow. (Taken in the workshops of NI Transformers Limited, Dundee.)*

Figure 10.7 *Typical temperatures in various parts of a large transformer when the temperature of the surrounding atmosphere is 20 °C. (Adapted from Figure 4.7 (page 121) Alternating Current Machines, M. G. Say, Longman Group UK, 1984.)*

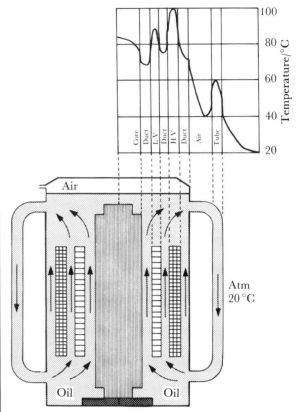

losses, and the windings rise in temperature. The thermal energy is transported by conduction, convection and radiation to the atmosphere.

Figure 10.6 shows a coil being wound for a large transformer. The conductor is not wire, but a copper strip with a rectangular cross-section; it is insulated by paper wrapped around it. The cylinder has strips of pressed fibre board laid along its length, and the windings are made over these strips. Thus channels are left between the cylinder and the coils; and when the unit is assembled upright in oil, the oil will be able to flow up the channels and cool the hot conductor.

Examine Figure 10.6 again. There are spacers between each turn, and the gaps enable cooling oil to surround each turn.

Figure 10.7 shows a longitudinal section of a large transformer. In the centre is the laminated core, of magnetically soft steel. From the core, working outwards, there are: a channel; the low-voltage windings; a channel; the high-voltage windings; a channel; the wall of the tank; the atmosphere; a cooling pipe; and the open atmosphere. Above a section of the transformer is a curve which gives typical temperatures for the parts when the atmospheric temperature is 20 °C.

Examine Figure 10.7 and the temperature distribution.

10.3 *A large transformer: temperatures and cooling.*

(a) In Figure 10.7, when the atmospheric temperature is 20 °C, what are the approximate

Figure 10.8 *A pole-mounted transformer with an oil-filled plain tank. Output power, 25 kW.*

Figure 10.9 *The transformer in Figure 10.8 supplies a remote farm. The supply arrives along 11 000 V lines and is transformed down to 240 V.*

temperatures of (i) the core; (ii) the low voltage windings; (iii) the high voltage windings?

(b) Draw a rough sketch of a side of the tank and a cooling tube, at a size rather larger than the diagram given in Figure 10.7. Using arrows, mark in air *convection currents* near the wall and tube. Suggest whether the higher air temperature will be between the wall and the tubes, or beyond the tubes. Does your suggestion correspond with the evidence given in the temperature distribution curve?

Look at Figures 10.8 and 10.9. They show a pole-mounted transformer. Such tranformers are used for supplying isolated farms and isolated groups of houses in country areas. They transform from either 11 000 V or 6600 V to 240 V. The smallest units provide about 15 kW of power, and the largest about 200 kW. Up to a power of about 25 kW a plain oil-filled tank is sufficient to provide cooling, but above about 25 kW, extra surface area is needed and side-tubes are added.

10.4 *A small transformer: convection and radiation.* A pole-mounted transformer of the type shown in Figure 10.8 is to provide 20 kW of power, with losses of 0.6 kW (that is, an efficiency of about 97%). The average temperature of the tank walls above atmospheric temperature is to be 35 K. If the tank is to be cubic in shape, of what length of side will it need to be?

Experiments with typical transformer tank

walls show that they can transfer to the atmosphere about 12.5 W of power per m² of tank surface for every 1 K of wall temperature above atmospheric temperature. (This figure is made up of 6.0 W by radiation and 6.5 W by convection.)

Proceed as follows: (a) What surface area of tank will be needed to transfer 600 W of power to the atmosphere, with a 35 K temperature difference? (b) What length of side of a cubic tank will be needed?

10.5 *A small transformer: convection and radiation.* A transformer has a tank surface area of 1.4 m² which is at an average temperature of 35 K above atmospheric temperature. The convection energy transfer coefficient, h, between the tank wall and air is $h = 6.5 \, \text{W m}^{-2} \, \text{K}^{-1}$. The emissivity of the tank surface is $\varepsilon = 0.9$, and the Stephan–Boltzmann constant is $\sigma = 5.7 \times 10^{-8}$ $\text{W m}^{-2} \, \text{K}^{-4}$. The atmospheric temperature is 17 °C.

(a) At what rate is energy being lost to the atmosphere by convection? (Use equation (2).)
(b) At what rate is energy being lost to the atmosphere by radiation? (Use equation (4).)
(c) What is the combined loss rate?

As the power of transformers increases, so the total losses increase and cooling pipes have to be added to the tanks. This adds greatly to the surface area for *convection*, but it makes no significant difference to the area available for *effective radiation*.

10.6 Why does adding cooling pipes to a transformer tank make no significant difference to the area available for effective radiation (that will actually contribute to cooling)? Suggestion: draw a rough sketch of the side of a tank with several cooling tubes; and draw in arrows to represent radiation from the tank and the tubes.

A very large transformer with a power output of 7.5 MW (7500 kW) had power losses of about 60 kW, which had to be transferred to the atmosphere. The tank was fitted with cooling tubes which together totalled over 900 m in length. The transfer to the atmosphere was: radiation, 9 kW; convection from the tank walls, 5 kW; and convection from the tubes, 46 kW; giving a total of 60 kW. The proportion of the total due to radiation was 9 kW/60 kW = 15%; and thus the proportion due to convection was 85%.

For a small pole-mounted transformer having a plain tank (with no tubes) the proportion due to radiation is

$$\frac{6.0 \, \text{W}}{(6.0 \, \text{W} + 6.5 \, \text{W})} = \frac{6.0 \, \text{W}}{12.5 \, \text{W}} = 48\%$$

and thus the proportion due to convection is 52%.

For small transformers with plain tanks, the transfer to the atmosphere is about half by radiation and half by convection. The larger a transformer becomes, the greater is the transfer by convection, until, with very large transformers, it is between 80% and 90% by convection.

Answer to text questions

10.1 (a) 4.9 kW; (b) Radiation.
10.2 (a) 2.6 kW; (b)(i) 4.9 kW; (ii) 2.6 kW; (iii) 7.5 kW.
10.3 (a)(i) 84 °C; (ii) 90 °C; (iii) 100 °C.
10.4 (a) 1.4 m²; (b) 0.48 m.
10.5 (a) 320 W; (b) 290 W; (c) 610 W.

11. Heating and cooling: heat capacity and latent heat

Figure 11.1 *A tank which is to contain a hot fluid. An insulated electrical heating element is being wound round the tank. Its functions will be, first, to raise the temperature of the cold contents, and then to maintain the high temperature. (Source: BICC Pyrotenax Limited, Hebburn, Tyne and Wear.)*

Heating and cooling of materials

In many industrial processes, particularly in the chemical industry, it is necessary to raise the temperature of materials. This requires energy, and therefore heat: a flow of energy.

This energy increases the *internal energy* of the material. Internal energy is made up of two parts: the *potential energy* in the interatomic and inter-molecular bonds; and the *kinetic energy* of the vibrations of the atomic particles in their crystal lattice or molecules, together with kinetic energy of translation in liquids and gases.

When energy is supplied to a solid so that its temperature rises, the lattice vibrations increase in magnitude. At some stage, the vibrations become so large that the lattice begins to break down; further supplies of energy contribute to further breaking down of the lattice and not to raising the temperature. The *temperature therefore remains constant*, and a transition from solid to liquid occurs. This phase change is *melting*, and the temperature at which it occurs is the *melting temperature*.

Once all the solid has melted, and all the material is in liquid form, further supplies of energy result in a raising of the temperature of the liquid. This continues until the vapour pressure of the liquid equals the pressure of the atmosphere over the liquid, at which point the liquid boils. Then further supplies of energy provide the particles with sufficient kinetic energy to escape from the surface of the liquid. Energy is *not* used in raising the temperature of the liquid. The temperature remains constant. This phase change from liquid to vapour is *boiling*, and the temperature at which it occurs is the *boiling temperature*.

The energy needed to convert the substance from solid to liquid is known as its *latent heat of fusion*; the energy needed to convert the material from liquid to vapour is known as its *latent heat of vaporisation*. When the *quantity of material is specifically 1 kg*, the quantities of energy are the *specific latent heat of fusion* and the *specific latent heat of vaporisation*.

A convenient measure of the energy required to raise the temperature of a substance (solid, liquid, or gas) would be the quantity of energy which is required to raise 1 kg of the substance through a temperature change of 1 K; this is known as the *specific heat capacity* of the substance.

The converse of each of these processes is that when a substance cools it gives out energy. If large quantities of material are involved, as they usually are in industry, particularly in the chemical industry, then special arrangements have to be made to remove the energy, to transfer it away from the material. An *energy exchanger* of some type will be needed.

Definitions

The *specific heat capacity*, c, of a substance is the quantity of energy required to raise the temperature of 1 kg of the substance through a temperature change of 1 K:

$$c = \frac{\Delta Q}{m\Delta\theta}, \quad \text{units, J kg}^{-1}\text{K}^{-1} \tag{1}$$

The *specific latent heat of fusion*, l_m, of a substance is the quantity of energy which is required to convert 1 kg of the solid into liquid at the same temperature.

$$l_\text{m} = \frac{\Delta Q}{m}, \quad \text{units, J kg}^{-1} \tag{2}$$

The *specific latent heat of vaporisation*, l_v, of a substance is the quantity of energy which is required to convert 1 kg of the substance from liquid to vapour at the same temperature:

$$l_\text{v} = \frac{\Delta Q}{m}, \quad \text{units, J kg}^{-1} \tag{3}$$

Rearranging equation (1) we have

$$c = \frac{\Delta Q}{m\Delta\theta} \qquad \Delta Q = cm\Delta\theta \tag{4}$$

If a substance having a mass, m, and a specific heat capacity, c, has to be raised through a temperature rise of $\Delta\theta$, the quantity of energy which is needed to do this is given by equation (4). Conversely, if the material is cooling through a temperature drop of $\Delta\theta$, then the quantity of energy which will be given out and which may have to be removed by an energy exchanger is given by equation (4).

Since a knowledge of the energy requirement will be needed for an industrial heating process, and since an appropriate size of energy exchanger will have to be designed in a cooling process, this equation, which relates energy change to temperature change, is in everyday use by engineers.

A power cable on short circuit

Figure 11.2 *A site engineer is examining a power cable for supplying power to machinery. The cable contains four insulated copper conductors, each able to carry a current of 190 A.*

The cable shown in Figures 11.2 and 11.3 is designed to carry a steady load current of 190 A, under which condition the conductors may be at a temperature of about 70 °C, depending on the external weather conditions. (The maximum allowable conductor temperature for XLPE insulation is 90 °C.) The cables, however, have to be designed and manufactured so as to be able to stand a short circuit current of large magnitude for a short time. This particular cable will safely carry a short circuit current of 10 000 A for a time of 0.5 s, or a short circuit current of 7000 A for 1 s. Such times are too short for the energy which is liberated in the conductor to be transferred through the insulation, and all the energy is taken up in raising the temperature of the conductor. The maximum conductor temperature which can be allowed for XLPE insulation is 250 °C under short circuit conditions of brief duration.

11.1 *Calculating the temperature rise of a conductor on short circuit.* Data for the copper conductor in one core of the cable in Figures 11.2 and 11.3 are: total cross-section area of the copper strands, 50 mm²; resistance per kilometre, 0.387 Ω; specific heat capacity, $c = 390\,\text{J kg}^{-1}\text{K}^{-1}$; density, 8900 kg m⁻³.

Figure 11.3 The structure of the cable in Figure 11.2 (approximately twice actual size). The insulation around each conductor is cross-linked polyethylene (XLPE). The armour is of strands of galvanised steel wire. The outer protective cover is of polyvinyl chloride (PVC). (Source: BICC Cables Limited, Wrexham.)

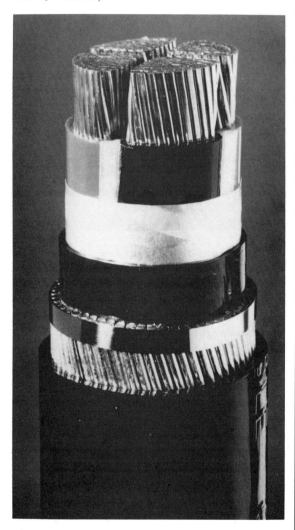

A short circuit current of 6000 A occurs and lasts for 1.0 second.

Calculate the rise in temperature of the conductor.

Proceed as follows:

(a) Refer to equation (4) for the relationship between energy supplied and temperature rise produced; and rearrange this to give $\Delta\theta$.

(b) Consider a 1 m length of conductor and find the energy which is liberated in 1 s (I^2R).

(c) Consider a 1 m length of conductor and find its mass, m.

(d) In the rearranged equation, which gives $\Delta\theta$, substitute values appropriately to find $\Delta\theta$.

A tank of solid paraffin wax

A chemical which is a solid at atmospheric temperatures may have to be used or processed in the liquid state, in which case it must be heated to the appropriate temperature. The company which manufactures the heating elements for tanks shown in Figure 11.1 provided the following example and data.

11.2 A tank was required which would, from time to time, store paraffin wax for a considerable period. The wax was fed into the tank in the hot liquid state; during storage it cooled to atmospheric temperature, and solidified. At a later date, when the wax was needed in liquid form, it had to be heated to the required temperature. The company was asked to provide suitable thermal insulation for the tank, and a suitable electrical heating element for the purposes of, first, heating the tank and contents from 10 °C to 95 °C and, then, maintaining the tank at that temperature during the process.

Calculate the *energy* that would have to be supplied to raise the temperature of the tank and its contents; and the *power* that would be required if the heating had to be achieved in 24 hours.

Data

The cylindrical tank
Dimensions = 1.20 m diameter × 1.37 m high;
Walls, base and cover: 5 mm thick mild steel plate;
Density, $\rho = 7800 \text{ kg m}^{-3}$;
Specific heat capacity, $c = 500 \text{ J kg}^{-1} \text{ K}^{-1}$.

The paraffin wax
Density, $\rho = 900 \text{ kg m}^{-3}$;
Specific heat capacity, $c = 2900 \text{ J kg}^{-1} \text{ K}^{-1}$
(for both solid and liquid wax);

Melting temperature, 56 °C;
Specific latent heat of melting, $l_m = 146\,000\,\mathrm{J\,kg^{-1}}$.

Required To raise the tank full of wax from 10 °C to 95 °C, in order to use the wax. Proceed as follows:

(a) Calculate the energy required to raise the steel tank from 10 °C to 95 °C.

(b) Calculate the energy required to raise the solid wax at 10 °C to its melting point at 56 °C.

(c) Calculate the energy needed to melt the wax, at its melting point of 56 °C.

(d) Calculate the energy needed to raise the temperature of the molten wax from 56 °C to 95 °C.

(e) Find the total energy needed.

(f) Find the power which the electric elements would have to provide if this energy were to be supplied in 24 hours.

Water and air cooling of machines

Figure 9.3 on page 84 shows the principles of water cooling in internal combustion engines, and Table 9.1 on page 85 shows useful work and losses for a diesel engine. Look again at the diagram and the table and read the text which relates to them.

11.3 In a diesel engine the water flow rate round the cylinders and then through the water to air energy exchanger ('radiator') was $1\,\mathrm{kg\,s^{-1}}$. The water temperatures at the top and bottom of the exchanger were 92 °C and 86 °C. (a) How much energy per second was being transferred to the atmosphere? (b) What was the power transfer? (Specific heat capacity of water, $c = 4200$ $\mathrm{J\,kg^{-1}\,K^{-1}}$.)

11.4 In another diesel engine the cooling water flow rate was $90\,\mathrm{kg\,min^{-1}}$, and the energy exchanger top and bottom water temperatures were 98 °C and 93 °C respectively. (a) What was the energy transfer to the atmosphere per second? (b) What was the power transfer to the atmosphere? (Specific heat capacity: see Question 11.3.)

Figure 11.4 *A small water pump unit which can be manoeuvred by hand. The pump is on the right. The one-cylinder, diesel, air-cooled engine that drives it is on the left; 10 kJ of energy per second must be removed from the engine by the cooling air.*

11.5 Examine the photograph and caption in Figure 11.4. The engine can deliver 5 kW of power along the shaft to the pump; but to keep the engine cool, 10 kW of power (10 kJ of energy per second) have to be removed by air blown over cooling fins. The rise in air temperature must be kept within a maximum of 40 K.

Calculate the air flow rate required to remove 10 kJ of energy per second with an air temperature rise of 40 K. Give the answer (a) in kg of air per second; and (b) in m^3 of air per minute. (Density of air, $\rho = 1.2\,\mathrm{kg\,m^{-3}}$; specific heat capacity of air, at constant pressure, $c = 1000\,\mathrm{J\,kg^{-1}\,K^{-1}}$).

11.6 Examine the photograph and caption in Figure 11.5. The currents in the rotor windings and in the stator windings produce I^2R losses which appear as heat; eddy currents in the core laminations also result in heat. From these causes energy is released in the alternator at the rate of $1.2\,\mathrm{kJ\,s^{-1}}$ (1.2 kW), and its temperature rises. Even with air cooling, the operating temperature of the coils is about 100 °C–120 °C, depending upon the atmospheric temperature.

Find the rate at which air must be drawn over the coils of the alternator by its internal fan, such that the rise in air temperature is 30 K. Give the answer (a) in $\mathrm{kg\,s^{-1}}$; (b) in cubic metres of air per minute. (Air data: at end of Question 11.5.)

Figure 11.5 *A mobile generator of ac, with a 5 kW output. The petrol engine is on the right. The cylindrical alternator is at lower left. The alternator windings are cooled by a forced stream of air, removing over 1 kJ of energy per second.*

Some industrial energy exchangers

Shell and tube exchangers

Most of the heating and cooling in a chemical plant, and in many other industrial situations, is in units called 'heat exchangers'. In fact, the process taking place is *energy transfer*, and the units might be called 'energy transfer units'; but the term 'heat exchanger' is firmly established and is used worldwide.

Figure 11.6 shows the principle of one of the most common types of exchanger: the 'shell and tube' exchanger. The fluid which is to be processed (this might be a liquid, a vapour or a gas, or very fine solid particles) is usually passed through the

Figure 11.6 *Shell and tube 'heat' exchangers. (a) One fluid passes through the tubes; the other passes over and around the tubes. (b) In order to ensure that the fluid in the shell passes over and along the whole length of the tubes, baffle plates are fitted to direct the flow of fluid.*

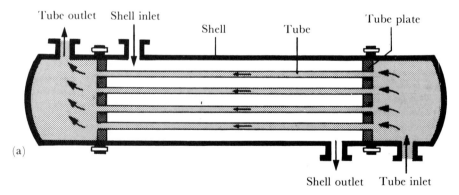

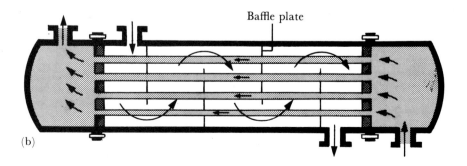

Figure 11.7 *Two shell and tube heat exchangers. Each exchanger has a shell with an external diameter of 0.5 m. In an exchanger, the tubes are $3\frac{1}{3}$ m in length and there are 370 of them, giving a total tube surface area of 62 m². (Source: Thermo Engineers Limited, Aylesbury.)*

Figure 11.8 *A partly assembled heat exchanger. Two tube plates with their tube ends are exposed. (Taken in the workshops of Alval Process Engineering Limited, Leven, Fife.)*

tubes. Another fluid is passed into the shell and over and around the tubes; this fluid will be hot if the purpose is to raise the temperature of the other fluid, and it will be cold if the purpose is to cool the other fluid.

In order to ensure that the shell-side fluid does not travel by an almost direct route diagonally across the shell to the shell outlet, and in order to ensure that it does flow as completely as possible over the whole length of the tubes, baffle plates are fitted down the length of the shell. These baffle plates extend at least half-way across the diameter of the shell, and often farther.

In a large exchanger there may be several hundred tubes.

Examine Figure 11.7, and read its caption. Find the shell inlet and outlet, and the tube inlet and outlet. These have all been sealed by cover plates which have been bolted on to prevent the entry of dust or other material during storage and delivery. Examine Figure 11.8 and read its caption.

11.7 *Energy transfer in a 'heat exchanger'.* An exchanger is to be used to heat water from 30 °C to 80 °C, and the water will flow through the tubes at a rate of 180 kg min⁻¹. The heating fluid is to be hot exhaust gases, which will be passed through the shell-side, entering at a temperature of 220 °C and leaving at a temperature of 120 °C. What flow rate of hot gases, in kg min⁻¹, will be needed to achieve the required heating of the water?

Proceed as follows:

(a) Find the energy required per minute to heat the water.

(b) Find the mass of exhaust gases which is needed to provide this energy. (Specific heat capacities: water, $c = 4200$ J kg⁻¹ K⁻¹; the exhaust gases, $c = 1000$ J kg⁻¹ K⁻¹.)

11.8 A small exchanger is to be used to cool hot oil, using water as the cooling fluid. The oil has to be cooled from 270 °C to 120 °C, and its flow rate will be 200 kg per hour. If the cooling water has a flow rate of 300 kg per hour and enters the exchanger at a temperature of 20 °C, at what temperature will the water leave the exchanger? (Specific heat capacities: oil, $c = 2100$ J kg^{-1} K^{-1}; water, $c = 4200$ J kg^{-1} K^{-1}.)

An evaporator

Evaporation is a very important process in the chemical industry. Weak solutions may have to be made more concentrated, and this will involve evaporating off some of the solvent. The temperature of the solution will have to be raised to its boiling point, requiring energy; the boiling liquid will then have to be evaporated, and more energy will be required to provide the *latent heat of vaporisation*. This second stage requires much more energy than the first stage, and the total energy required in an industrial evaporation can be very large, and therefore very expensive.

It is therefore very important that the process is designed so as to make the most efficient possible use of energy; this involves using hot vapour and hot liquids several times over, in successively cooler stages, until as much energy as possible has been recovered from them and used.

Figure 11.9 shows the principles of a typical industrial evaporator. Examine the diagram and read the caption. Refer back to Figure 11.6 and compare the two exchangers.

Figure 11.9 *Structure of a typical industrial evaporator. It is a modified shell and tube exchanger, which is mounted vertically. In the basic exchanger in Figure 11.6 there are two inlets and two outlets. There is a third outlet in the evaporator, for the vapour. (Modified from a diagram, Alval Process Engineering Limited, Leven, Fife.)*

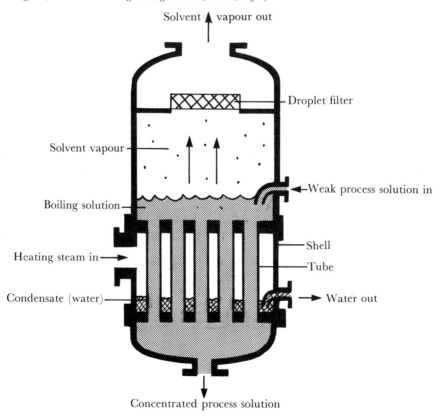

11.9 In Figure 11.9: (a) find the tubes; (b) find the shell; (c) what goes in at the tube inlet? (d) what comes out at the tube outlet? (e) what is the source of heat for the process? (f) what happens to this substance, and in what form does it leave the exchanger? (g) where does the boiling take place?

The evaporator in Figure 11.9 is shown as being heated by steam, but other substances can be used. The steam condenses on the tube walls, giving out latent heat of condensation; and the energy from this phase change (vapour to liquid) boils the solution in the tubes. As the latent heat of vaporisation of water is $l_v = 2260 \text{ kJ kg}^{-1}$, when 1 kg of steam condenses to water 2260 kJ of energy are released; this is a large quantity of energy.

In Figure 11.9, as the weak process solution boils in the tubes and above them, vapour from the solvent is driven off and passes out through the top of the exchanger. The solution becomes more concentrated, and concentrated solution passes out of the bottom of the exchanger.

Part of the manufacturing process when producing cotton fabrics is to treat the cotton with sodium hydroxide solution. This strengthens the fabric and makes the fibres more receptive to dyeing. Figure 11.10 shows the evaporator flow and control systems for evaporating weak sodium hydroxide solution and producing a more concentrated solution.

The evaporation takes place in three stages, using three evaporators. The evaporation is conducted under reduced pressure, using a vacuum pump. The heating is done by steam.

Figure 11.10 *Evaporator flow and controls diagram for concentrating a weak solution of sodium hydroxide in the mercerising process in the production of cotton fabrics. Figures with no units are kg per hour, e.g. 11 000 is 11 000 kg per hour; PI, pressure indicator; TI, temperature indicator; FI, flow indicator; R, recorder; C, controller, e.g. FRC, flow recorder and controller. (Source: Alval Process Engineering Limited, Leven, Fife.) (This diagram may be copied for class use.)*

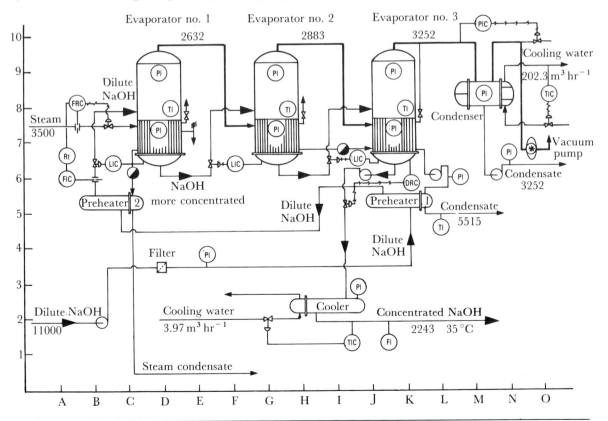

Since the 'weak process solution' is an aqueous solution of sodium hydroxide, the *solvent is water*; the solvent vapour which is driven off by evaporation is *water vapour*, and this emerges through the top of the evaporator.

Examine the evaporation system. Proceed as follows.

1. Take a preliminary look at Figure 11.10; and read the caption and the key to the letters for the controls.
2. Examine Evaporator No. 1. Heating steam enters from the left, and goes into the shell. The condensate of hot water leaves the shell at the bottom left of it. (This hot water then goes to an exchanger to heat up incoming cool liquid: Preheater 2.)

    Dilute sodium hydroxide enters on the left, into the space above the tubes. It is boiled in and above the tubes, and flows down, energing from the bottom of the exchanger as a more concentrated solution.

    At the top of the evaporator solvent vapour emerges, that is, water vapour. It does so at a flow rate of 2632 kg per hour.
3. Find the concentration that has taken place. The *dilute* sodium hydroxide solution enters the plant at the bottom left of the drawing, at grid reference A2; and it does so at a flow rate of 11 000 kg per hour. The *concentrated* solution leaves the plant at the bottom right of the drawing, at L2; and it does so at a flow rate of 2243 kg per hour. The solution has therefore lost water. It has lost (11 000−2243) kg per hour, which is 8757 kg per hour, by evaporation.

    The solid which was originally contained in 11 000 kg of solution is now contained in only 2243 kg of solution, and the solution is thus much more concentrated. It has approximately 11 000/2243 times the original concentration, that is, about 5 times that concentration.
4. Follow the route of the sodium hydroxide solution. The dilute sodium hydroxide solution enters the plant at A2. Its route is marked by broad arrows. Follow its route, and consider what is happening at each stage.

5. A mass balance. The mass of materials that enter the plant per hour must equal the mass of materials that leave it per hour.

    Obtain a mass balance for the sodium hydroxide solution. Set out the masses as follows:

Mass of solution IN per hour $TOTAL = \ldots$ kg
Process stages:
Evaporator No. 1, D10   Evaporate off . . . kg
Evaporator No. 2, G10   Evaporate off . . . kg
Evaporator No. 3, K10   Evaporate off . . . kg

Total evaporated off . . . kg
Concentrated NaOH solution OUT . . . kg

TOTAL OUT . . . kg

6. Energy recovery. Find two units in the plant where a hot outgoing fluid is being used to warm up a cool incoming fluid.
7. Cooling. Find an exchanger where cooling water is being used. How is the flow of cooling water being regulated?

Because of the very wide range of substances that have to be processed in the chemical industry, many different designs of evaporator are in use.

Answers to text questions

11.1 80 K.
11.2 (a) 12 MJ; (b) 186 MJ; (c) 204 MJ; (d) 158 MJ; (e) 560 MJ; (f) 6.5 kW.
11.3 (a) 25 kJ s^{-1}; (b) 25 kW.
11.4 (a) 31 or 32 kJ s^{-1}; (b) 31 or 32 kW.
11.5 (a) 0.25 kg s^{-1}; (b) 13 m^3 min^{-1}.
11.6 (a) 0.04 kg s^{-1}; (b) 2.0 m^3 min^{-1}.
11.7 (a) 38 MJ; (b) 380 kg min^{-1}.
11.8 70 °C.
11.9 (c) Weak process solution; (d) Concentrated process solution; (e) Steam; (f) It condenses to water, and leaves as water; (g) In the tubes, and in the solution above them.

12. *Thermal insulation in buildings: U-values*

Routes of heat losses in buildings

Figure 12.1 Main heat loss routes in an uninsulated house. The financial cost by each route is for each £100 of total cost.

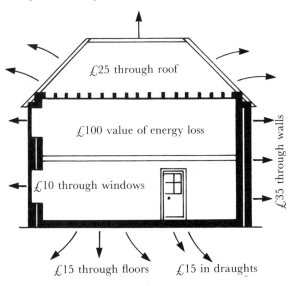

Figure 12.2 A cavity wall being built for a house. A block of insulation material has been placed in the cavity space. The cavity will be filled with such blocks.

In order to maintain the temperature inside a building, energy which is lost from the interior to the outside must be replaced. This has to be done by means of a heating system, and the energy which it provides costs money. An average three- or four-bedroom house which is uninsulated or poorly insulated can lose energy worth several hundreds of pounds each year. Large offices and factories and other places of work can lose tens of thousands of pounds each year in this way.

The main routes of heat loss from a building are through the walls, the roof, the floor and the windows; for a house it is in that order. Figure 12.1 shows diagrammatically the breakdown of a £100 cost of heat losses in a house, by the principal routes.

Since the main loss route is through the walls, it is very important to reduce this loss. The photograph given in Figure 12.2 shows a cavity wall being built for a house. The cavity is being filled with blocks of insulation material, which will reduce the loss to one-third of the uninsulated value.

The UK Building Regulations

In order to ensure certain minimum standards in the construction of houses, offices, factories and other buildings for the benefit of their users, successive governments have arranged the drawing up and publication of Building Regulations. These are legal requirements, and architects and construction firms are required to design and build at least to the standards given in the Regulations.

The following are extracts from the Regulations.

PART J. CONSERVATION OF FUEL AND POWER

The intention of this Part is to ensure that effective measures are incorporated in a building for the conservation of fuel and power ... The requirements in the Technical Standards set out energy conservation measures for the building fabric and the building services.

The standards for the building fabric require the provision of energy measures to limit the heat losses and, where appropriate, to maximise heat gains. The standards can be met in three different ways:

(a) The Elemental Approach. Under this method every part of the floors, walls and roofs of a building must be constructed to meet the prescribed U-values; and the total area of windows and rooflights must not exceed prescribed limits.

[This is then followed by methods (b) and (c), which are omitted here.]

The standards for the building services require the provision of certain measures: heating and hot water services must be fitted with appropriate automatic controls; and pipes, ducts, and hot water storage vessels (e.g. hot water cylinders) must be thermally insulated.

Thermal transmittance in structures: U-values

What are U-values?

Energy flows through a composite structure, such as a double wall with a cavity, by several different modes: conduction, convection, and radiation.

A convenient way of quantifying the overall contribution of a structural element (a window, door, wall or roof) to the loss of energy from a building would be to obtain figures for *the rate at which energy flows through a 1 m² cross-section of the structure and is lost per square metre of external surface.* Figure 12.3 shows the principle. Read the caption and study the diagram.

If the window in Figure 12.3(a) had a total area of $1\frac{1}{2}$ m², the rate of energy loss would be 90 W, or 90 J s^{-1}. In (b), if the interior of the room were at a temperature of 20 °C, the rate of energy loss would be 10 W per square metre of wall surface.

This energy has been *transmitted through the structure*, and has been lost from 1 m² of surface. In comparing structures as transmitters of thermal energy, a convenient temperature difference between the inner and outer faces would be *unit temperature difference, 1 K*.

Thus for the window glass in Figure 12.3(a), the rate at which energy is transmitted through the thickness of the glass and lost from the surface is 60 W m^{-2}/10 K, or 6 W m^{-2} per 1 K temperature difference, 6 W m^{-2} K^{-1}. This is known as the *U-value* of the glass: its *overall thermal transmittance coefficient*.

The U-value of a material or of a structure is the rate at which energy is transmitted through 1 m² of it per 1 K temperature difference between its faces.

The overall thermal transmittance coefficient, U, of the composite wall in Figure 12.3(b) is

$$U = \frac{5 \text{ W}}{1 \text{ m}^2 \times 10 \text{ K}} = 0.5 \text{ W m}^{-2} \text{ K}^{-1}$$

$$U = \frac{Q/t}{A \times \Delta\theta} \tag{1}$$

From which,

$$\frac{Q}{t} = UA \times \Delta\theta \tag{2}$$

From equation (2), for a given area of surface, A, and a given temperature difference, $\Delta\theta$, between its sides, a low rate of energy loss will be achieved if U is low. Thus, from the point of view of the insulation of buildings, external structural units should have low U-values. Examine Figure 12.4 from this point of view.

Figure 12.3 *Two structural units of a building, with an interior temperature of 10 °C and an exterior temperature of 0 °C. (a) A sheet of standard window glass; the rate of energy loss from 1 m² of surface is 60 W, or 60 J s⁻¹. (b) A double brick wall with an insulated cavity, and plaster internally; the rate of energy loss from 1 m² of surface is 5 W.*

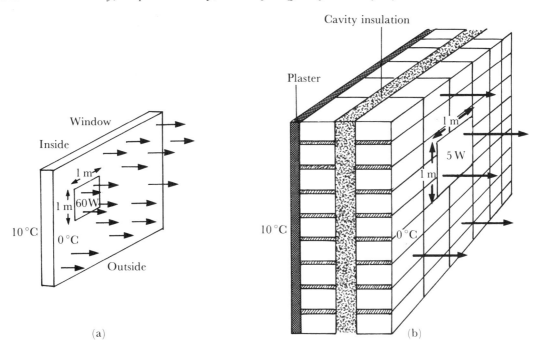

Figure 12.4 *U-values (W m⁻² K⁻¹). These diagrams show the U-values of some units in buildings.*

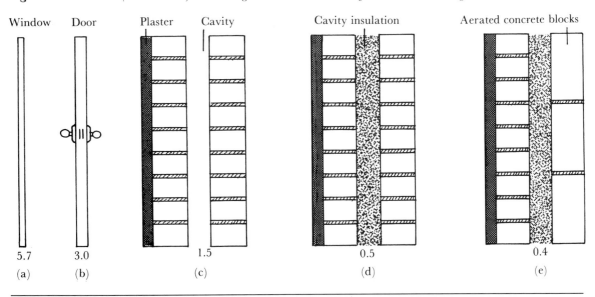

Insulation materials in buildings

The insulation used in construction is made from a very wide variety of raw materials, but almost all forms of insulation make use of the same principle: that of trapping very large numbers of small pockets of air in a matrix of a solid. In a small pocket, air is stationary. Under these circumstances it can only transfer energy by conduction, and its thermal conductivity, k, is very low:

$k = 0.026\,\mathrm{W\,m^{-1}\,K^{-1}}$ (see Table 10.1).

Examples of such materials are

- Rigid materials: aerated concrete blocks (load bearing); fibreglass slabs and mineral wool slabs (non-load bearing). See Figure 12.2.
- Flexible materials: fibreglass rolls and mineral wool rolls, for unrolling between joists in roof insulation. See Figure 12.5.
- Loose fill materials: Expanded polystyrene granules, mineral wool blown into a wall cavity.

Reflective materials, such as aluminium foil, are also used to reflect radiation back towards the interior of the building.

Figure 12.5 shows a flexible roll of mineral wool insulation being laid in a roof space. Figure 12.6

Figure 12.5 *A mineral wool roll being laid between joists in a roof space. (Source: Rockwool Limited, Bridgend, Mid Glamorgan.)*

Figure 12.6 *The microstructure of a mineral wool insulation; air is trapped between the fibres. (Source: Rockwool Limited.)*

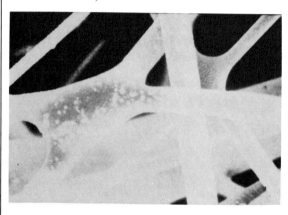

shows the microstructure of the wool. The manufacturer describes its manufacture and nature as follows.

> *'Rockwool' is manufactured from a volcanic rock to which coke and limestone are added. The mixture is melted, and the molten material is spun into wool which is then resin impregnated. This material forms the basis for a wide range of products including loose wool, rolls, mats, slabs, and laminates.*
>
> *The mineral wool consists principally of silicon oxide together with a number of metal oxides. (Rockwool Limited)*

The microstructure of the wool traps pockets of air. Examine Figure 12.6 and confirm that the *microstructure* traps air. Examine Figure 12.2 again to confirm that the *macrostructure* of layers of wool, bound by resin, also traps air.

Insulation materials have very low values of thermal conductivity; see Table 10.1 on page 91. For 'Rockwool' rolls and slabs the values are $k = 0.037\,\mathrm{W\,m^{-1}\,K^{-1}}$ and $0.033\,\mathrm{W\,m^{-1}\,K^{-1}}$ respectively.

How are U-values determined?

Most of the structures for which *U*-values are needed are *composite structures*, for instance, a wall (brick, insulation, concrete, plaster); for a suspended ground floor, a design common in Scotland (hardcore, damp proof membrane, air space, floor joists and insulation, floorboards); or for a flat roof (concrete, screed, insulation, weatherproof covering).

U-values are calculated from the thermal conductivity, *k*, and the thickness, *l*, of each of the components in the structure. The thermal conductivity is readily obtained experimentally. Tables are published giving the thermal conductivity for all types of standard construction materials; and the manufacturers of insulation materials provide *k* values as part of their product information. Knowing the thicknesses of the layers in the composite, and knowing their *k* values, the *U*-value of the composite may be calculated.

Using U-values

Figure 12.7 shows the maximum *U*-values acceptable in the United Kingdom for the design and construction of houses. They are: ground floor exposed to the atmosphere, 0.45; ground floor on solid ground, 0.45; walls, 0.45; roofs (sloping; dormer roof; and in roof spaces, the ceiling and sloping roof combined), 0.25 (*U*-values, $\mathrm{W\,m^{-2}\,K^{-1}}$).

Figure 12.7 U-*values* $(W\,m^{-2}K^{-1})$. *The maximum U-values acceptable for the parts of the fabric of a house are shown. (Adapted from Building Regulations.)*

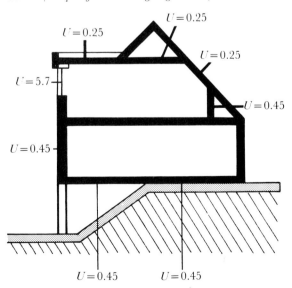

Figure 12.8 *A semidetached dwelling. With a knowledge of U-values, heat losses can be calculated. (Reproduced from British Standards, BS5250: 1989.)*

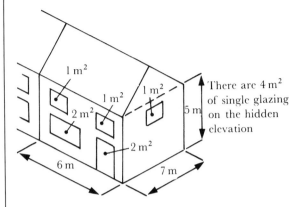

The Building Regulations require that the total window area should be limited. It must not exceed 15% of the total floor area.

12.1 *Acceptable window area.* Is the design for the window area in the house in Figure 12.8 acceptable under the UK Building Regulations (less than 15% of the total floor area)? Assume that the back of the house is the same as the front

12.2 *Heat losses through the windows.* The *U*-value of windows with single glazing is taken to be $5.7\,\mathrm{W\,m^{-2}\,K^{-1}}$. In the house shown in Figure 12.8, if the average inside temperature was to be 20 °C, and if the outside temperature was 0 °C, what would be the rate of loss of energy through the windows? Assume that the back of the house is the same as the front.

12.3 *Heat losses through the walls.* For the house in Question 12.2, calculate the rate of energy loss through the walls. (Ignore the gable end, which is above the ceiling insulation.) *U*-value of walls, $0.45\,\mathrm{W\,m^{-2}\,K^{-1}}$.)

12.4 *Heat losses through the roof.* For the house in Question 12.2, calculate the rate at which energy is lost through the roof. Use the ceiling area, and a *U*-value of $0.25\,\mathrm{W\,m^{-2}\,K^{-1}}$ for the combination of ceiling and roof.

12.5 *Heat loss through the floor.* For the house in Question 12.2, calculate the rate at which energy is lost through the floor. (Temperature of ground beneath the floor, $5\,^\circ$C; the U-value of the floor, $0.45\,\mathrm{W\,m^{-2}\,K^{-1}}$.)

Answers to text questions

12.1 Yes (10.7%).
12.2 1.0 kW.
12.3 0.72 kW.
12.4 0.21 kW.
12.5 0.28 kW.

13. The cooling of electronic devices

All electric conductors, components and equipment rise in temperature when they carry a current. This is a consequence of the nature of a current in a conductor. Energy which is used in forcing the electrons along the conductor against its resistance raises the internal energy of the conductor, with a consequent rise in its temperature. The energy which is released per second is given by the product (current × potential drop across the device); it is an I^2R loss.

If the temperature rises to a value that is too high, the components may be damaged, and insulation may be damaged. This is particularly true of semiconductor junctions. Germanium devices can operate up to a temperature of about 100 °C, and silicon devices to about 175 °C; but above these temperatures the junctions begin to disintegrate. Moreover, the higher the operating temperature of a semiconductor, the shorter is its life. Approximately, the life expectancy halves for every 10 K rise in temperature. Further, the electrical properties of a semiconductor (such as its threshold voltage) change with temperature, and for certain key electronic devices it may be necessary to arrange for them to operate within a particular temperature range.

Thus for semiconductor devices there are three important reasons for preventing an undesirable temperature rise: at raised temperatures the life decreases, the electrical properties change, and above about 175 °C the junction begins to disintegrate.

Arrangements for cooling semiconductor devices in electronic equipment are therefore of fundamental importance. The principal method is by the use of metal 'heat sinks'.

Figure 13.1 shows a range of different shapes and sizes of heat sinks. Energy released in the junction area of a device is carried by *conduction* through the device to its case; by *conduction* from the

Figure 13.1 *A range of heat sinks for cooling electronic devices such as diodes and transistors. (Heat sinks supplied by Redpoint Limited, Swindon.)*

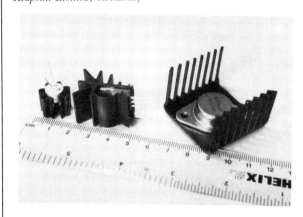

case to the heat sink; and by *conduction* along the metal of the heat sink. From the heat sink surface it is lost to the surroundings by *convection* and *radiation*.

Heat sinks are usually made of aluminium, which has a high value of thermal conductivity. The surface is usually blackened to increase its emissivity, and so increase its effectiveness as a radiator.

Figure 9.4 shows equipment for producing very high-quality dc from ac; it contains several heat sinks. Look at this photograph to see an example of heat sinks in use.

In the photograph given in Figure 13.2 a power transistor for circuit board mounting is fitted into a heat sink. The performance curves in (c) are for two sizes of this style of heat sink, each with the same cross-sectional shape and size, but one being 20 mm long and the other being 35 mm long.

13.1 If a transistor is fitted in a 20 mm long sink of the type shown in Figure 13.2 and if in operation it loses 4 W of power as heat ($4\,\mathrm{J\,s^{-1}}$), what is the rise in temperature at the centre of the heat sink above the surroundings?

Figure 13.2 *Details of a small heat sink for circuit board mounting: (a) heat sink for cooling the power transistor clipped in it; (b) cross-section of the heat sink (actual size); (c) performance curves for sinks of 20 mm and 35 mm length. ((b) and (c), and the heat sink sample in (a): Redpoint Limited, Swindon.)*

(a)

(b)

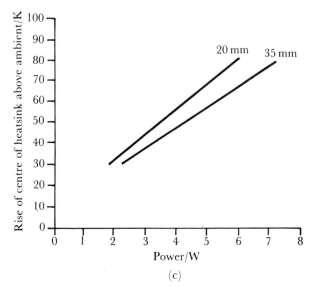

(c)

13.2 If the same transistor in the same use as in Question 13.1 were fitted in a 35 mm long sink, what then would be the rise in temperature at the centre of the sink?

If the device is in a cabinet which contains a number of other power semiconductors, each producing heat, the temperature of the air in the cabinet could be at 35 °C or 40 °C. With the centre of the heat sinks at approximately 50 K above this ambient temperature, the case of the device would be at about 90 °C; and the interior of the device, containing the junction, would be higher still. In many instances, cabinets containing power semiconductors have to be air-cooled by forced convection, using fans.

Heat sinks themselves may have to be cooled by forced convection, particularly when the energy transfer rate is high.

Figure 13.3 shows an extruded aluminium heat sink for dissipating energy at rates of up to 250 W. It can be fitted with a cover and provided with a fan to produce forced air convection cooling along the channels between the fins. Examine the diagrams and photographs and read the captions.

The improvement to the cooling which is provided by the fan can be seen from the following data for a sink of length 100 mm. The temperature rise at the centre of the sink which is produced by 1 W of power dissipated is: with *natural* air cooling, 0.65 K; with *forced* air cooling, 0.16 K.

In a situation where 100 W have to be dissipated, the temperature rises would be 65 K and 16 K respectively.

Answers to text questions

13.1 55 K.
13.2 46 K or 47 K.

Figure 13.3 *Information about a heat sink which can be provided with forced convection air cooling: (a) cross-section of the body, showing the metal cooling fin pattern; (b) a power transistor mounted on the sink; the sink is 230 mm in length; (c) performance graph for two different lengths of sink (100 mm and 230 mm); (d) the sink has been fitted with a cover and a fan. (Source: Redpoint Limited, Swindon.)*

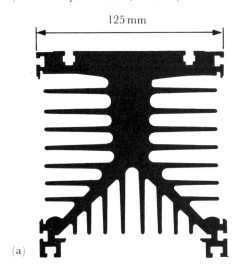

(a)

(b)

(c)

(d)

Index